Kaplan Publishing are constantly finding new ways to make a difference to your studies and our exciting online resources really do offer something different to students looking for exam success.

This book comes with free MyKaplan online resources so that you can study anytime, anywhere. **This free online resource is not sold separately and is included in the price of the book.**

Having purchased this book, you have access to the following online study materials:

CONTENT	AAT	
	Text	Kit
Electronic version of the book	✓	✓
Progress tests with instant answers	✓	
Mock assessments online	✓	✓
Material updates	✓	✓

How to access your online resources

Kaplan Financial students will already have a MyKaplan account and these extra resources will be available to you online. You do not need to register again, as this process was completed when you enrolled. If you are having problems accessing online materials, please ask your course administrator.

If you are not studying with Kaplan and did not purchase your book via a Kaplan website, to unlock your extra online resources please go to www.mykaplan.co.uk/addabook (even if you have set up an account and registered books previously). You will then need to enter the ISBN number (on the title page and back cover) and the unique pass key number contained in the scratch panel below to gain access. You will also be required to enter additional information during this process to set up or confirm your account details.

If you purchased through Kaplan Flexible Learning or via the Kaplan Publishing website you will automatically receive an e-mail invitation to MyKaplan. Please register your details using this email to gain access to your content. If you do not receive the e-mail or book content, please contact Kaplan Publishing.

Your Code and Information

This code can only be used once for the registration of one book online. This registration and your online content will expire when the final sittings for the examinations covered by this book have taken place. Please allow one hour from the time you submit your book details for us to process your request.

D0177120

Please scratch the film to access your MyKaplan code.

Please be aware that this code is case-sensitive and you will need to include the dashes within the passcode, but not when entering the ISBN. For further technical support, please visit www.MyKaplan.co.uk

KAPLAN

PUBLISHING

AAT

AQ2016

PROFESSIONAL DIPLOMA IN ACCOUNTING

Synoptic Assessment 2019

FAMILIARISATION AND PRACTICE KIT – RUBY DALE LTD

This practice kit supports study for the following AAT qualifications:
AAT Professional Diploma in Accounting – Level 4
AAT Level 4 Diploma in Business Skills
AAT Professional Diploma in Accounting at SCQF – Level 8

KAPLAN

PUBLISHING

British Library Cataloguing-in-Publication Data

A catalogue record for this book is available from the British Library.

Published by:

Kaplan Publishing UK

Unit 2 The Business Centre

Molly Millar's Lane

Wokingham

Berkshire

RG41 2QZ

ISBN: 978-1-78740-538-7

© Kaplan Financial Limited, 2019

Printed and bound in Great Britain.

This Product includes content from the International Ethics Standards Board for Accountants (IESBA), published by the International Federation of Accountants (IFAC) in 2015 and is used with permission of IFAC.

CONTENTS

Live assessment pre-release material

This practice kit is based on the live assessment pre-release information for Ruby Dale Ltd. Make sure you download and print a copy from the AAT website to use in conjunction with this kit.

Studying this material will encourage you to think about the assessment topics in an integrated way, which is necessary for performing well in the synoptic assessment.

Note: Kaplan authors have invented scenarios and additional details when writing questions based on Ruby Dale Ltd. When sitting the live assessment, make sure you don't confuse what content is in the pre-release information and what additional details are in this practice kit.

You will find a wealth of other resources to help you with your studies on the AAT website:

www.aat.org.uk/

Quality and accuracy are of the utmost importance to us so if you spot an error in any of our products, please send an email to mykaplanreporting@kaplan.com with full details, or follow the link to the feedback form in MyKaplan.

Our Quality Co-ordinator will work with our technical team to verify the error and take action to ensure it is corrected in future editions.

SYNOPTIC ASSESSMENT

AAT AQ16 introduces a Synoptic Assessment, which students must complete if they are to achieve the appropriate qualification upon completion of a qualification. In the case of the Advanced Diploma in Accounting, students must pass all of the mandatory assessments and the Synoptic Assessment to achieve the qualification.

As a Synoptic Assessment is attempted following completion of individual units, it draws upon knowledge and understanding from those units. It may be appropriate for students to retain their study materials for individual units until they have successfully completed the Synoptic Assessment for that qualification.

Four units within the Professional Diploma in Accounting are mandatory. Of these, three are assessed individually in end of unit assessments, but this qualification also includes a synoptic assessment, sat towards the end of the qualification, which draws on and assesses knowledge and understanding from all four mandatory units:

- Financial statements of Limited Companies – end of unit assessment

- Management Accounting: Budgeting – end of unit assessment

- Management Accounting: Decision and Control – end of unit assessment

- Accounting Systems and Controls – assessed within the synoptic assessment only

Summary of learning outcomes from underlying units which are assessed in the synoptic assessment

Underlying unit	Learning outcomes required
Accounting Systems and Controls	LO1, LO2, LO3, LO4
Financial Statements of Limited Companies	LO1, LO5
Management Accounting: Budgeting	LO3
Management Accounting: Decision and Control	LO1, LO2, LO4, LO5

KAPLAN PUBLISHING

FORMAT OF THE ASSESSMENT

The specimen synoptic assessment comprises six tasks and covers all six assessment objectives. Students will be assessed by computer-based assessment. Marking of the assessment is partially by computer and partially human marked.

In any one assessment, students may not be assessed on all content, or on the full depth or breadth of a piece of content. The content assessed may change over time to ensure validity of assessment, but all assessment criteria will be tested over time.

The following weighting is based upon the AAT Qualification Specification documentation which may be subject to variation.

	Assessment objective	Weighting
AO1	Demonstrate an understanding of the roles and responsibilities of the accounting function within an organisation and examine ways of preventing and detecting fraud and systemic weaknesses.	20%
AO2	Evaluate budgetary reporting; its effectiveness in controlling and improving organisational performance.	15%
AO3	Evaluate an organisation's accounting control systems and procedures.	15%
AO4	Analyse an organisation's decision making and control using management accounting tools.	15%
AO5	Analyse an organisation's decision making and control using ratio analysis.	20%
AO6	Analyse the internal controls of an organisation and make recommendations.	15%
	Total	100%

Time allowed: 3 hours

PASS MARK: The pass mark for all AAT assessments is 70%.

 Always keep your eye on the clock and make sure you attempt all questions!

The detailed syllabus and study guide written by the AAT can be found at:

www.aat.org.uk/

INDEX TO QUESTIONS AND ANSWERS

EXAM TECHNIQUE

- **Do not skip any of the material** in the syllabus.

- In particular, make sure you are comfortable with **assumed knowledge** from other papers at this level and those from lower levels.

- Make sure you are **familiar** with the live assessment pre-release information and have read through it at least twice.

- **Read each question** *very* carefully.

- **Double-check your answer** before committing yourself to it.

- Answer **every** question – if you do not know an answer to a multiple choice question or true/false question, you don't lose anything by guessing. Think carefully before you **guess**.

- If you are answering a multiple-choice question, **eliminate first those answers that you know are wrong.** Then choose the most appropriate answer from those that are left.

- **Don't panic** if you realise you've answered a question incorrectly. Getting one question wrong will not mean the difference between passing and failing.

Computer-based exams – tips

- Do not attempt a CBA until you have **completed all study material** relating to it.

- On the AAT website there is a CBA demonstration. It is **ESSENTIAL** that you attempt this before your real CBA. You will become familiar with how to move around the CBA screens and the way that questions are formatted, increasing your confidence and speed in the actual exam.

- Be sure you understand how to use the **software** before you start the exam. If in doubt, ask the assessment centre staff to explain it to you.

- Questions are **displayed on the screen** and answers are entered using keyboard and mouse. At the end of the exam, in the case of those units not subject to human marking, you are given a certificate showing the result you have achieved.

- In addition to the traditional multiple-choice question type, CBAs will also contain **other types of questions**, such as number entry questions, drag and drop, true/false, pick lists or drop down menus or hybrids of these.

- In some CBAs you will have to type in complete computations or written answers.

- You need to be sure you **know how to answer questions** of this type before you sit the exam, through practice.

KAPLAN'S RECOMMENDED REVISION APPROACH

QUESTION PRACTICE IS THE KEY TO SUCCESS

Success in professional examinations relies upon you acquiring a firm grasp of the required knowledge at the tuition phase. In order to be able to do the questions, knowledge is essential.

However, the difference between success and failure often hinges on your exam technique on the day and making the most of the revision phase of your studies.

The **Kaplan Study Text** is the starting point, designed to provide the underpinning knowledge to tackle all questions. However, in the revision phase, poring over text books is not the answer.

Kaplan Pocket Notes are designed to help you quickly revise a topic area; however you then need to practise questions. There is a need to progress to exam style questions as soon as possible, and to tie your exam technique and technical knowledge together.

The importance of question practice cannot be over-emphasised.

The recommended approach below is designed by expert tutors in the field, in conjunction with their knowledge of the examiner and the specimen assessment.

You need to practise as many questions as possible in the time you have left.

OUR AIM

Our aim is to get you to the stage where you can attempt exam questions confidently, to time, in a closed book environment, with no supplementary help (i.e. to simulate the real examination experience).

Practising your exam technique is also vitally important for you to assess your progress and identify areas of weakness that may need more attention in the final run up to the examination.

In order to achieve this we recognise that initially you may feel the need to practice some questions with open book help.

Good exam technique is vital.

THE KAPLAN REVISION PLAN

Stage 1: Assess areas of strengths and weaknesses

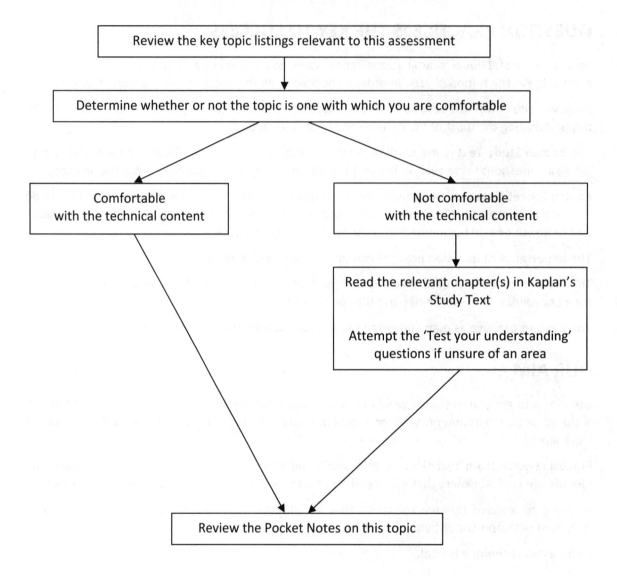

Review the key topic listings relevant to this assessment

Determine whether or not the topic is one with which you are comfortable

Comfortable with the technical content

Not comfortable with the technical content

Read the relevant chapter(s) in Kaplan's Study Text

Attempt the 'Test your understanding' questions if unsure of an area

Review the Pocket Notes on this topic

Stage 2: Familiarisation and practice questions

Follow the order of revision of topics as presented in this practice kit and attempt the questions in the order suggested.

Try to avoid referring to Study Texts and your notes and the model answer until you have completed your attempt.

Review your attempt with the model answer and assess how much of the answer you achieved.

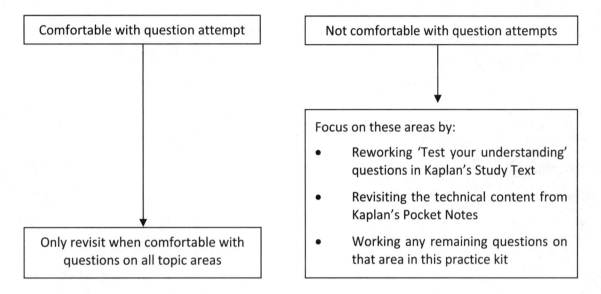

Stage 3: Final pre-exam revision

We recommend that you **attempt at least one mock examination** containing a set of previously unseen exam-standard questions based on the live assessment pre-release information.

Attempt the mock CBA online in timed, closed book conditions to simulate the real exam experience.

Also ensure that you have worked through the two sample assessments carefully and thought how to answer the same questions from the perspective of the company in the live pre-seen release.

Section 1

COMMENTARY ON LIVE PRE-RELEASE INFORMATION

1 ADVANCED PRE-RELEASE INFORMATION

INSTRUCTIONS TO CANDIDATES

This material is designed to contextualise the tasks you will receive in your live assessments.

This document has been made available to you ahead of your assessment. Studying this material will encourage you to think about the assessment topics in an integrated way, which is necessary for performing well in the synoptic assessment.

You will not be able to take a copy of this document into the assessment with you. However, you will have access to this material through pop-up windows in the assessment.

COMPANY BACKGROUND

History

Ruby Dale Ltd is a private limited company based in Manchester, which designs, manufactures, distributes and retails luxury shoes and handbags.

The business began 10 years ago when Ruby Dale, an award winning fashion school graduate, started to sell her bespoke hand-made shoes on the internet on a made to order basis.

Ruby was joined two years later by Jack Carey, an entrepreneur, and together they formed Ruby Dale Ltd. Jack had seen Ruby's shoes featured in a leading fashion magazine and, sensing their wider market appeal, wished to manufacture a ready-to-wear version of the shoes on a much greater scale. They built a factory on an industrial estate in Manchester to make the shoes, and opened their first shop in Manchester in 20X0.

Recent developments

Ruby Dale Ltd has expanded rapidly over the last few years – facilitated by numerous celebrity endorsements – more than doubling the workforce and opening three new shops in London, Paris and New York, one in each location. The company also supplies its products to major high street retailers and independent stores, as well as enabling customers to purchase directly through the company's website. As Ruby Dale Ltd has grown it has diversified its portfolio of products, and now complements its core offering of luxury women's shoes with handbags, men's evening shoes and luxury trainers. The handbag collection in particular now forms an integral part of the business in terms of helping to promote the Ruby Dale lifestyle brand. In the last year, the company has also re-launched the made-to-order service – having originally stopped this when the shoes first started to be mass produced – to allow customers the option of purchasing a product that will be bespoke to them.

Financial performance

Revenue increased by 20% in the year ending 30 September 20X5, with women's shoes – comprising 80% of turnover – being the main driver as the company launched a number of new styles across its product range. While sales to customers in the United Kingdom and Europe largely remained unchanged, due to economic uncertainty caused by political events. Sales to customers in Asia, the USA and the emerging economies, such as Brazil and Russia, experienced strong growth, assisted by a weaker pound sterling, rising levels of disposable income and a greater brand awareness. Sales to UK customers still remain the company's main market, representing 42% of turnover. The e-commerce part of the business performed particularly well, delivering exceptional sales growth of 34%, as Ruby Dale Ltd introduced new features and technology on the online platform to improve the shopping experience of customers.

Resources

On 30 September 20X5 Ruby Dale Ltd had 160 employees.

Department	Number of staff
Production, storage and distribution	73
Retail	41
Administration	26
Marketing	12
Design and development	8

Apart from 29 employees who work in the company's four shops, the rest are located at Ruby Dale Ltd's headquarters in Manchester where production is based. Although the site has expanded in order to meet the growing demand for the company's products, it is now starting to reach the limit of its manufacturing capacity with a couple of product lines experiencing temporary stock-out shortages in the early part of 20X5. After a comprehensive tendering process, Ruby Dale Ltd made the decision in the latter part of the year to outsource production of its handbags to a manufacturing company located in Asia, its principal area of market growth. Further outsourcing opportunities are also to be considered as the company looks to reduce its cost base and further expand its product range.

SUSTAINABILITY

Ruby Dale Ltd is committed to sustainable development with regard to the economic, social and environmental aspects of its business.

The company operates a comprehensive training programme for all employees, which allows it to advance workplace safety, productivity and satisfaction. This is especially important given the large influx of new members of staff. It has recently embarked on an apprenticeship scheme to develop the company's designers and managers of the future, and works closely with local schools and colleges to promote interest in the fashion industry and to identify high potential talent. In 20X3 Ruby Dale Ltd set up the Ruby Dale Foundation which sponsors under-privileged children to study fashion at university, as well as raising funds for local community projects.

In relation to the environment, Ruby Dale Ltd is striving to achieve ambitious savings in water, waste and energy. Recent initiatives include the installation of a water recycling system in the factory; removing single-use plastic items such as plastic bags, water bottles and cutlery from all company sites; replacing traditional lighting with LED lights; upgrading the fabric of buildings to improve insulation and boost energy efficiency.

In addition, Ruby Dale Ltd has now implemented a scheme whereby faulty goods returned by customers are donated to charity wherever possible for resale on the second hand market rather than sent to landfill. The company also works closely with suppliers to ensure that all materials are sourced using sustainable methods and staff are paid a fair wage and have good working conditions.

SWOT ANALYSIS

Joshua Edeki (Finance Director) has prepared the following SWOT analysis to evaluate Ruby Dale Ltd's competitive position:

Strengths

- Talented design team

- Dedicated management with lots of experience of working in the fashion goods sector

- trong relationships with both suppliers and customers

- Globally recognised brand

Weaknesses

- Limit reached on current in-house manufacturing capacity

- Diseconomies of scale arising as a consequence of the larger workforce, for example communication issues, loss of co-ordination and low staff motivation

- Internal control weaknesses as a result of controls not evolving in step with the growing business

- Risk of overtrading

Opportunities

- Diversify further the product range, for example into eyewear, fragrance, watches and jewellery

- Open new shops to achieve a greater high street presence, for example in the growing markets of Asia and the emerging economies

- Outsource production to overseas manufacturers

- Float on the stock market to obtain additional finance to fund investment

Threats

- Downturn in the macro-economic environment which would impact upon the demand for luxury products

- Rise in the cost of materials

- Aggressive competitive action taken by other companies in the luxury goods sector in respect of poaching customers and obtaining prime retail sites

- Adverse market reaction to new product lines

Section 2

PRACTICE QUESTIONS

TASK 1.1

Assessment objective 1	Demonstrate an understanding of the roles and responsibilities of the accounting function within an organisation and examine ways of preventing and detecting fraud and systemic weaknesses.

1   STATUTORY DUTY

Who has the statutory duty to prepare accounts for Ruby Dale?

The company auditors.	
The directors of the company.	
Joshua Edeki, Finance Director.	
Erika Tordoff, Financial Controller.	
Companies House.	

2   RESPONSIBILITY

Who is responsible for maintaining sound risk management and internal control systems within Ruby Dale?

The company auditors.	
The directors of the company.	
Joshua Edeki, Finance Director.	
Erika Tordoff, Financial Controller.	
Companies House.	

10   INFORMATION SYSTEM CONTROLS

Information system controls can be classified as 'security controls' and 'integrity controls'.

Drag and drop the following controls into the correct category.

	Security	Integrity
Locked doors		
Passwords		
Batch totals		
Reconciliation		
CCTV		
Check digits		
Authorisation of data entry		
Fire alarms		

11   PURCHASE CYCLE CONTROLS 1

Ruby Dale has experienced occasions when payment was made for goods not received.

Which TWO of the following controls in a purchase cycle could be implemented to reduce the risk of payment of goods not received?

Sequentially pre-numbered purchase requisitions and sequence check.	
Matching of goods received note with purchase invoice.	
Goods are inspected for condition and quantity and agreed to purchase order before acceptance.	
Daily update of inventory system.	

12   PURCHASE CYCLE CONTROLS 2

Ruby Dale has experienced occasions when unnecessary goods and services were purchased.

Which TWO of the following controls in the purchase cycle could be implemented to reduce the risk of procurement of unnecessary goods and services?

Centralised purchasing department.	
Sequentially pre-numbered purchase requisitions and sequence check.	
Orders can only be placed with suppliers from the approved suppliers list.	
All purchase requisitions are signed as authorised by an appropriate manager.	

13   EXPENSE CLAIM CONTROLS

Harry Grisham has been appointed as the new IT manager at Ruby Dale. Harry really enjoys the job and even though the remuneration is not great, the other managers at the company have explained the way they 'get around' that issue. The sales manager explains to Harry that the key is to 'put everything on expenses – private petrol, drinks and even clothing. It's all fine and as long as you have a receipt, no-one in the finance department will question it'. He continues that 'It's fine because the board are aware of it and turn a blind eye'.

Which ONE of the following essential internal control measures is evidently missing?

Ruby Dale lacks a control environment as the board are not setting an ethical tone at the top.	
Ruby Dale lacks an Internal Audit department.	
Ruby Dale lacks an experienced finance manager.	
Ruby Dale lacks an external auditor.	

14   PASSWORDS 1

You have been asked to set up a password for Ruby Dale's accounting system.

Which of the following would be the most secure?

24june1963	
LaraJo	
mypassword	
Qwerty123!#	

15   PASSWORDS 2

You have been asked to set up a new system of passwords for Ruby Dale's accounting system.

Which TWO of the following would reduce the effectiveness of passwords?

Requirement that passwords are changed every two weeks	
Users are allowed to choose their own passwords	
Automatic lock-out after 3 failed attempts to access system	
Making the sharing of passwords a disciplinary offence	
Displaying the password on the screen when entered	

16   INTERNAL CONTROLS 1

An internal control system in an organisation consists of five components: the control environment, the risk assessment process, the information system, control activities and monitoring of controls.

Match each of the following activities to the component that it illustrates.

	Control environment	Information system	Control activities
The process of preparing the financial statements			
Locking the inventory storeroom			

17   INTERNAL CONTROLS 2

Ruby Dale is looking at introducing new internal controls to help reduce the risk of fraud.

Match each of the following activities to the type of control that it illustrates.

	Authorisation	Information processing	Physical control
The financial controller will count petty cash on a weekly basis			
There will be two keys to a locked safe: one held by the FD and the other by the MD.			

18   INTERNAL CONTROLS 3

Ruby Dale is looking at introducing new computer controls to reduce payroll fraud. Computer controls can be described as "general" and "application".

Match each of the following activities to the type of computer control that it illustrates.

	General	Application
Storing extra copies of programs and data files off-site		
New programmes to check data fields on input transactions		
Manual checks to ensure that input data were authorised		
Password protection limiting access to data		
Range checks on payroll processing		
Manual checks to ensure that timesheets are authorised before details are processed		

19 INTERNAL CONTROLS 4

Ruby Dale is looking at introducing new internal controls but the directors are concerned that even the best controls still have limitations.

Indicate whether the following limitations are true or false.

	True	False
The cost of implementing controls may be more expensive than the benefits gained due to reduced risk		
The effectiveness of many controls rely on the integrity of those applying them		
Internal controls are only applied to material items so smaller items remain unchecked		
Standard controls may not be designed to deal with unusual transactions		

20 FRAUD 1

Erika Tordoff is concerned that some Ruby Dale staff may be misappropriating customer remittances.

Which THREE of the following control activities would best prevent this fraud occurring?

Segregation of duties between cash handling and recording	
Post opening by two people	
Investigation of differences between website sales and cash banked	
Regular banking of cash and cheques received in the post	

21 FRAUD 2

Given high staff turnover and low morale within Ruby Dale, the financial controller is worried that fictitious employees could be included on the payroll by a dishonest employee from the accounts department.

Which ONE of the following control activities would best prevent this occurring?

Payroll standing data periodically printed out and checked on a line-by-line basis to independently held employee details	
Use of hierarchical passwords over standing data files	
Pre-authorisation of all amendments to payroll standing data by an independent official	
Supervision of the wages pay out by an independent official	

Conclusion – whether or not the budget is realistic

24 RUBY DALE BUDGETING PROCESS

Ruby Dale is about to undertake the next annual budgeting cycle. The different managers involved have been provided with guidance notes to help them with this.

Ruby Dale Budgeting Guidance (extracts)

Inflation:

Inflation should be allowed for when appropriate. For wages, rent costs and materials costs inflation, production managers can select between the RPI (retail price index) and the CPI (consumer price index which excludes mortgage payments). Both these indexes measure past inflation in the United Kingdom where Ruby Dale is based.

No guidance is given about inflation of other costs.

Marketing:

The overall marketing budget is set by head office without consultation with other sales managers. Ruby Dale has sales managers who have responsibility for different products, markets and customers – for example, Gill Evans works with two major retailers within the UK, whereas Jenni Black is responsible for website sales.

Each year the total marketing budget is set, taking account of the specific products that Ruby Dale wishes to promote. No account is taken of the previous year's spend. However, it is up the other sales managers to then estimate what effect this marketing spend might have on their areas of interest.

The marketing department provide sales trend analysis based on regression analysis, which produces a straight-line relationship between the marketing spend and sales volumes for previous periods.

Provide a 'SWOT' analysis of the above budget process and recommend, where appropriate changes to this process. **(15 marks)**

Note:

A 'strength' is where you feel the process is good and a 'weakness' is where you feel the process is not so good. An 'opportunity' to improve the process may exist in places and a 'threat' is best written as a bad consequence of a poor budget process.

Strengths

Weaknesses

Opportunities

Threats

TASK 1.3

Assessment objective 3	Evaluate an organisation's accounting control systems and procedures.

Note: in the two sample assessments task 1.3 only asked for weaknesses and explanations of implications. In the two tasks here, we have also asked for recommendations as this is also useful practice for task 6.

25 RUBY DALE'S PURCHASING SYSTEM

Below is a description of the purchasing and payments system for Ruby Dale in respect of manufacturing costs in its factory.

Ordering

Whenever new materials are required, such as leather to make shoes, the relevant department within the factory sends a requisition form to the ordering department. An order clerk raises a purchase order and contacts a number of suppliers to see which can despatch the goods first. This supplier is then chosen. The order clerk sends out the purchase order. This is not sequentially numbered and only orders above £1,000 require authorisation.

Bookkeeping

Purchase invoices are input daily by the purchase ledger clerk, who has been in the role for many years and, as an experienced team member, he does not apply any application controls over the input process. Every week the purchase day book automatically updates the purchase ledger, the purchase ledger is then posted manually to the general ledger by the purchase ledger clerk.

Payments

Ruby Dale maintains a current account and a number of saving (deposit) accounts. The current account is reconciled weekly but the saving (deposit) accounts are only reconciled every two months.

In order to maximise their cash and bank balance, Ruby Dale has a policy of delaying payments to all suppliers for as long as possible. Suppliers are paid by a bank transfer. The finance director is given the total amount of the payments list, which he authorises and then processes the bank payments.

Required:

Identify and explain FOUR deficiencies in the system, explain the possible implication of each deficiency and provide a recommendation to address each deficiency.   (15 marks)

Weakness	Implication	Recommendation

26   RUBY DALE'S SALES AND INVENTORY PROCESSES

Ruby Dale's website allows individuals to order shoes and bags directly, and full payment is taken in advance. Currently the website is not integrated into the inventory system and inventory levels are not checked at the time when orders are placed.

Goods are despatched via local couriers; however, they do not always record customer signatures as proof that the customer has received the goods. Over the past 12 months there have been customer complaints about the delay between sales orders and receipt of goods. Ruby Dale has investigated these and found that, in each case, the sales order had been entered into the sales system correctly but was not forwarded to the despatch department for fulfilling.

Ruby Dale also has business customers – mainly high street retailers – who undergo credit checks prior to being accepted and credit limits are set accordingly by sales ledger clerks. These customers place their orders through one of the sales team, who decides on sales discount levels.

Materials are purchased from a wide range of suppliers. As a result of staff changes in the purchase ledger department, supplier statement reconciliations are no longer performed. Additionally, changes to supplier details in the purchase ledger master file can be undertaken by purchase ledger clerks as well as supervisors.

In the past six months Ruby Dale has changed part of its warehousing process and as a result some new equipment has been purchased, however, there are considerable levels of equipment that are now surplus to requirement. Purchase requisitions for all new equipment have been authorised by warehouse supervisors and little has been done to reduce the surplus of old equipment.

Required:

In respect of the internal control of Ruby Dale's sales and inventory processes, identify FIVE deficiencies, explain the possible implication of each deficiency and recommend a control to address each of these deficiencies. **(15 marks)**

Weakness	Implication	Recommendation

Weakness	Implication	Recommendation

27 RUBY DALE'S INVENTORY COUNTING PROCESSES

Each winter, Ruby Dale is obliged to count its inventory in its factory and distribution warehouse.

This year Ruby Dale arranged for an internal auditor to attend some of the inventory counts and feedback their findings. It was hoped that this would lead to improved procedures in the future. In one location within the factory, the local staff were short numbered and so the internal auditor acted as a counter and an auditor at the same time.

In the warehouse, pre-printed inventory sheets were produced which showed the designated bin location of all inventory lines and the staff were instructed to record the number of items that they found of each inventory line in each location.

The warehouse was split into 8 zones with two teams being responsible for 3 zones each and then, depending on how fast each team counted the other two zones could be dealt with.

Suppliers were requested not to deliver during the centralised warehouse counts. This policy was mostly followed but one supplier of claps for handbags failed to obey and a large delivery was made. The driver offloaded the stock in the car park and left so as not to interfere with the counting process.

During the count, large boxes of leather not yet unpacked were not opened but the slips on the side of the boxes were used to note the contents on the inventory sheets.

A note was made of damaged items but, since the Financial Controller had already done a slow-moving inventory calculation (see task 6 for the details), old inventory was not recorded.

Outline 5 weaknesses and their effect on the accounting systems in the boxes below:
(15 marks)

Weakness	Effect of Weakness

Weakness	Effect of Weakness

TASK 1.4

Assessment objective 4	Analyse an organisation's decision making and control using management accounting tools.

28   PRODUCTION DECISIONS

The company is now starting to reach the limit of its manufacturing capacity with a couple of product lines experiencing temporary stock-out shortages in the early part of 20X5. After a comprehensive tendering process, Ruby Dale Ltd made the decision in the latter part of the year to outsource production of its handbags to a manufacturing company located in Asia, its principal area of market growth. Further outsourcing opportunities are also to be considered as the company looks to reduce its cost base and further expand its product range.

However, the directors are still concerned that, until sufficient outsourcing has been successfully implemented, there will still be times in the near future when the factory will be fully utilised and want to formulate a plan so that production managers know how best to allocate scarce resources such as skilled production labour. At the latest Board meeting there was disagreement how best to make decisions.

All men's shoes are manufactured using the same two production lines in the Manchester factory. Making and finishing the shoes to the required quality is very labour intensive and the availability of this skilled labour represents the most significant capacity constraint for Ruby Dale. The following table provided shows the sales and profitability of four potential designs of men's shoes for the forthcoming month.

Sales and profitability data

Car model	A	B	C	D
Potential sales demand (units)	250	300	200	400
	£	£	£	£
Selling price	150	120	125	100
Variable costs	100	80	70	50
Contribution per unit	**50**	**40**	**55**	**50**
Total contribution	12,500	12,000	11,000	20,000
Apportioned fixed overheads	(5,000)	(6,000)	(4,000)	(8,000)
Operating profit	**7,500**	**6,000**	**7,000**	**12,000**
Skilled labour time per unit (minutes)	100	96	120	110
Contribution per minute	**0.50**	**0.42**	**0.46**	**0.45**

Notes:

1 Discounts have been excluded from the above selling prices.

2 Fixed overheads relate to costs associated with ordering, distribution and central warehouse costs. These are apportioned on a unit basis.

Directors' discussion

At the Board meeting, the directors of Ruby Dale gave their views as to which of the four shoes should be made if skilled labour was limited.

Ruby Dale, the Managing Director, argued that, based on total operating profits, shoe D should be stocked. Her argument was that the apportioned fixed overhead had to be taken into account as it had to be covered somewhere in the business.

Nadia Bibi, the Sales Director, disagreed. Her opinion was that the allocated fixed costs were irrelevant and that they should just look at the contribution, although she was unclear whether it was better to look at contribution per unit (and pick C) or total contribution (and pick D).

Mark Austin, the Production Director, thought the correct approach was to look at the contribution per minute as they had limited skilled labour, rather than the total or unit contribution. He thus favoured stocking shoe A.

(a)   **BRIEFLY discuss the validity of each of the three directors' views on how the final decision should be made as to which shoes to make.**   **(9 marks)**

Managing Director

Sales Director

Production Director

(b)   **BRIEFLY explain TWO other factors should be taken into consideration before making a final decision.**   **(6 marks)**

Factor 1

Factor 2

29   NEW SUPPLIERS

Ruby Dale is considering extending the range of suppliers it uses for outsourcing the manufacture of some bags and has short-listed three potential candidates.

The decision is to be based on a range of factors, both financial and non-financial.

The financial argument will be based simply on cost. Ruby Dale is keen to introduce target costing to achieve a minimum 60% mark up and it is felt that suppliers should be chosen that help Ruby Dale achieve this.

Non-financial factors will focus on quality – both that of the product offered and the quality of the service provided.

To help collect information for making the decision, one of the most popular bags, a university-style leather satchel, will be used as an example. The satchels are available in a range of sizes and colours. Ruby Dale currently uses double stitching throughout for added strength, along with steel buckles, although brass buckles are used on the specialist premium lines.

(a)   Which of the following prices should be used for target costing?   **(2 marks)**

The budgeted price that Ruby Dale has set for 20X6	
The existing price that Ruby Dale uses	
The market average price	
The price charged by Ruby Dale's main competitor for a similar bag	

(b)   Calculate the target cost for a large leather satchel using the information below.

(3 marks)

Cost per unit	£
Production cost (charged by supplier)	
Transportation costs (paid by Ruby Dale)	5.50
Total cost	
Mark up (60%)	
Target selling price	165.00

(c) **Briefly explain how the concept of value analysis applies to Ruby Dale and the options available to it to close any cost gap.** **(4 marks)**

Value analysis
Options available to Ruby Dale

(d) **Information for three potential suppliers of the satchel is given as follows:**

Supplier	A	B	C
Production cost	£100.00	£90.00	£80.00
Offers price discounts for bulk orders	Yes	No	No
Typical delivery time (weeks)	3	4	7
Typical credit terms (days)	30	60	45
Double stitching used throughout	Yes	Yes	No
Material used for buckles	Brass	Steel	Plastic

Discuss which supplier should be chosen by referring to both financial and non-financial factors. **(6 marks)**

Financial factors

Non-financial factors

30 RUBY PORTFOLIO PLANNING

The sales of one of Ruby Dale's designer shoe ranges – a shoe based on those made for and worn by a celebrity at the Oscars ceremony in February 2017 – has been in steady decline and questions are being raised about its long-term future.

The shoes are packaged in a special presentation box, retail at £250 a pair and Ruby Dale makes a contribution margin on sales of 60% on this product. This margin only accounts for variable costs. If fixed costs are averaged over all products than this product's share would be £25,000 a quarter. It is not thought that there is any directly attributable fixed cost.

The reason for the decline is thought to be because the celebrity concerned has significantly changed their "look" and pictures on social media show them wearing very different styles of shoes to the range being sold. The shoe is only sold via the website.

To help assess the decision to discontinue the range, data has been gathered by the sales team on the volume of sales of the engines concerned over the past two years split by quarters (8 quarters in total) and your help is being requested to provide interpretation of that data.

The data analysis was performed using regression techniques where:

$$Y = a + bX$$

Y is the sales volume and X is the relevant quarter number

The data started with quarter 2 in 2017 (Q = 1) and provided six quarters of data (up to Q = 6). The 'b' value was found to be −20 and the 'a' value was 345 units

(a)   Using the data above complete the following table: **(7 marks)**

Quarter Number	Volume units	Revenue £	Variable Cost £	Contribution £
1 (Q2 2017)	350			
2 (Q3 2017)	290			
3 (Q4 2017)	266			
4 (Q1 2018)	258			
5 (Q2 2018)	246			
6 (Q3 2018)	238			
7 (Q4 2018)				
8 (Q1 2019)				
9 (Q2 2019)				
10 (Q3 2019)				

(b)   Briefly discuss the meaning of the value 'b' above and your findings using the data and comment on whether Ruby Dale, from a financial viewpoint, would want to continue to supply this product up to and including quarter 3 2019   (6 marks)

(c) Briefly discuss any non-financial considerations regarding the withdrawal of a particular range from sale. **(2 marks)**

TASK 1.5

Assessment objective 5	Analyse an organisation's decision making and control using ratio analysis.

31 RUBY DALE AND OVERTRADING

Erika Tordoff has expressed concerns that Ruby Dale's high growth rate (20% growth in revenue in 20X5) may result in an overtrading position, where its financial and other resources are insufficient for the rate of expansion.

To help assess the extent of this risk a range of ratios have been calculated to create a scorecard based on Ruby Dale's forecast performance for 20X6.

These are given below, together with some ratios from 20X5.

(a) Complete the scorecard by calculating the missing ratios. **(10 marks)**

RUBY DALE Scorecard	Y/e 30/9/X6	Y/e 30/9/X5
Profitability and gearing		
Gross profit %	58.4%	62.7%
Operating profit %	16.6%	%
Return on capital employed	11.8%	%
Gearing (debt/equity)	0.65×	0.55×
Liquidity ratios		
Current ratio	2.8:1	2.2:1
Acid test/Quick ratio	2.1:1	:1
Working capital days		
Inventory holding period	75 days	days
Trade receivables collection period	45 days	42 days
Trade payables payment period	60 days	74 days
Working capital cycle	86 days	days

(b)   Select the **ONE** correct observation about each aspect of business performance below.   (10 marks)

Profitability

20X6 will be a year of steady, if unspectacular, progress. Although margins have dipped, the return on capital employed has been kept constant.	
The changes in gross margin could be due to cost control problems concerning distribution.	
Increased competition and the resulting pressure on prices could explain the change in each of the three profitability ratios.	

Gearing

The increased gearing ratio proves that Ruby Dale has no problems raising additional debt finance.	
It is likely that the interest cover ratio has increased.	
The increased gearing ratio shows that the shareholders' position has become more risky.	

Liquidity

Both ratios have increased, which indicates that the company is less solvent.	
A higher quick ratio is a clear indicator of overtrading.	
The change in both the current and quick ratios could be partly explained by the increase in the receivables period.	

Working capital

The working capital cycle has worsened. This increases the possibility of Ruby Dale overtrading.	
There is a welcome improvement in the working capital cycle, mainly due to the change in the payment period for payables.	
The working capital cycle is worse than a year ago because of the change in inventory days.	

Overall performance

Despite overall growth, Ruby Dale is having a difficult year in 20X6 and needs to investigate why key ratios are deteriorating.	
20X6 looks to be a disaster for Ruby Dale.	
There is no evidence of possible control problems.	

32   RUBY DALE – COMPETITOR ANALYSIS

Joshua Edeki, the Finance Director, is preparing a presentation for the board of directors to discuss possible control problems within the business. He has asked you to complete a comparative 'score card' of key financial ratios comparing Ruby Dale and one of its main rivals, which he will use as part of his presentation.

Relevant data has been extracted for Ruby Dale as follows.

Extracts from accounts of Rival	Y/E 30/09/20X5
	£000
Profitability	
Sales revenue	13,945
Cost of sales	7,070
Profit from operations	1,325
Assets	
Non-current assets	3,559
Inventories	1,162
Trade receivables	1,233
Total	**5,954**
Equities and liabilities	
Equity	3,958
Non-current liabilities – loans	792
Trade payables	581
Bank overdraft	423
Tax liabilities	200
Total	**5,954**

(a)   Complete the scorecard by calculating the missing ratios.   **(10 marks)**

Y/e 30/09/X5	Ruby Dale	Rival
Profitability		
Gross profit %	62.7%	
Operating profit %	17.8%	9.5%
Return on capital employed	12.9%	
Liquidity ratios		
Current ratio	2.2:1	
Acid test/Quick ratio	1.3:1	0.6:1

Y/e 31/12/X5	Ruby Dale	Rival
Working capital days		
Inventory holding period	89 days	60 days
Trade receivables collection period	42 days	32 days
Trade payables payment period	74 days	
Working capital cycle	57 days	

(b)   Assess the following statements concerning potential control problems and indicate whether they are true or false.   **(10 marks)**

Statement	True	False
The difference in gross margins could be explained by the Rival giving excessive discounts in "sales" to shift excess inventory.		
If Ruby Dale has delayed paying suppliers at the year end, then this would contribute to the difference in current ratios.		
The difference in the lengths of the working capital cycles could be explained by a credit controller at Ruby Dale being off work due to illness.		
A warehouse employee in Ruby Dale was found to have stolen bags and sold them on an online auction site. This would contribute to the difference in the ROCE figures.		
Inadequate controls over expense claims for managers within Ruby Dale could contribute to the difference in the operating margins figures.		

33   CASH AND PROFIT

The directors of Ruby Dale have been having a discussion on the financial ratios of the business and which should take priority for the business.

Ruby Dale (Managing Director) stated "All that seems to matter is profit and profit-based ratios. Every time I watch a business program on television, profit is pretty much the first thing that is talked about." It is for this reason that I have instructed the accounts department to delay the payment of our next rent bill. This should increase our profitability at a vital time as I am meeting the bank soon to discuss future funding.

Mark Austin (Production Director) in part agreed but added "I feel that cash flow and liquidity ratios are also vital. However, at the end of the day cash and profit seem to be the same thing. I spend money on materials or wages and the same figure ends up in the profit and loss account, so if we are profitable we must have more cash coming in that going out."

Joshua Edeki (Finance Director) is a little despairing of his friends and colleagues and has asked you summarise the issue of 'profits versus cash' for him to use at the next board meeting where he will attempt to explain.

Briefly explain the profits and cash issues mentioned above under the following headings:

Why is profit important in business?	(5 marks)

Why must cash also be considered in business?	(5 marks)

Does the cash equal the profit?	(5 marks)

Discuss whether delaying the rent payment will be effective in increasing profits and the ethical stance the accounting department should take to the request. (5 marks)

TASK 1.6

Assessment objective 6	Analyse the internal controls of an organisation and make recommendations.

34 RUBY DALE'S INVENTORY STOCK TAKE

You have been asked to review the arrangements for Ruby Dale's year-end inventory count to be undertaken at the central warehouse on 30 September 20X6, which happens this year to be a Saturday. This will be a working day, so there will continue to be movements of new shoes, bags and raw materials in and out of the warehouse during the count. These will be kept to a minimum where possible.

The different categories of shoes and bags are stored within the first 20 aisles of the warehouse. Materials and components for the factory are stored in the last 10 aisles.

The following arrangements have been made for the inventory count:

The warehouse manager will supervise the count as he is most familiar with the inventory. There will be five teams of counters and each team will contain two members of staff, one from the finance department and another one volunteered from head office. None of the warehouse staff, other than the manager, will be involved in the count.

Each team will count an aisle of goods by counting up and then down each aisle. As this process is systematic, it is not felt that the team will need to flag areas once counted. Once the team has finished counting an aisle, they will hand in their sheets and be given a set for another aisle of the warehouse. In addition to the above, to assist with the inventory counting, there will be two teams of counters from the internal audit department and they will perform inventory counts.

The count sheets are sequentially numbered, and the product codes and descriptions are printed on them but no quantities. If the counters identify any inventory which is not on their sheets, then they are to enter the item on a separate sheet, which is not numbered. Once all counting is complete, the sequence of the sheets is checked and any additional sheets are also handed in at this stage. All sheets are completed in ink.

Sometimes the packaging for shoes can be damaged to such an extent it is not possible for them to be sold except at a discount. Also, some materials and components can become obsolete as the shoes or bags concerned become replaced and outdated due to changes in fashion. Any damaged or obsolete items identified by the counters will be left where they are but the counter is to make a note on the inventory sheets detailing the level of damage.

For the inventory count arrangements of Ruby Dale identify and explain FIVE deficiencies; and provide a recommendation to address each deficiency. **(15 marks)**

Deficiency	Recommendation

35   RUBY DALE'S SALES AND DESPATCH SYSTEM

As a result of poor customer feedback over service levels, Mark Austin (Production Director) has started to investigate in detail where the problems are arising. He is reasonably happy over the way stores and independent retailers are dealing with customers but has concerns over telephone and website transactions.

Other than through stores, sales orders are mainly placed through Ruby Dale's website but some are also made via telephone.

Online orders are automatically checked against inventory records for availability; telephone orders, however, are checked manually by order clerks after the call. A follow-up call is usually made to customers if there is insufficient inventory. When taking telephone orders, clerks note down the details on plain paper and afterwards they complete a three part pre-printed order form. These order forms are not sequentially numbered and are sent manually to both despatch and the accounts department.

As the company is expanding, customers are able to place online orders which will exceed their agreed credit limit by 10%. Online orders are automatically forwarded to the despatch and accounts department.

A daily pick list is printed by the despatch department and this is used by the warehouse team to despatch goods. The goods are accompanied by a despatch note and all customers are required to sign a copy of this. On return, the signed despatch notes are given to the warehouse team to file.

The sales quantities are entered from the despatch notes and the authorised sales prices are generated by the invoicing system. If a discount has been given, say for supplying a used cartridge, then this has to be manually entered by the sales clerk onto the invoice.

Due to the expansion of the company, and as there is a large number of sale invoices, extra accounts staff have been asked to help out temporarily with producing the sales invoices. Normally it is only two sales clerks who produce the sales invoices.

Identify and explain FIVE deficiencies in Ruby Dale's sales and despatch system and provide a recommendation to address each of these deficiencies.   **(15 marks)**

Deficiency	Recommendation

Deficiency	Recommendation

36   RUBY DALE'S GENERAL LEDGER SYSTEM

Ruby Dale's general ledger is controlled by Joshua Edeki (Finance Director/FD) and Erika Tordoff (Financial Controller or FC) with either of these people able to make independent journal entries. Joshua and Erika are friends and keen walkers and do like to get away over the autumn period to trek in various parts of the world. This isn't always easy to arrange as the year-end work needs to finish quickly to enable this holiday to take place. Nadia Bibi (Sales Director/SD) is given access to the general ledger over this period in the unlikely event further adjustments are needed.

Joshua does not require prior sight of the journals prepared by Erika as there is considerable trust between the two.

Anyone with general ledger access can create new general ledger accounts.

New slow moving inventory accounting policy

During the current year, the approach taken to accounting for slow moving inventory has been investigated by Joshua. As fashion changes then the level of inventory for some shoes and bags needed also change and this can sometimes leave Ruby Dale with unsaleable items. When this happens, a provision is made to reflect the potential loss held within inventory. Joshua has long felt that the existing approach was excessively prudent. The current approach is that when monthly sales of a line drop to below 50% of the previous year's monthly average, then all remaining inventory is written down to 50% of their value effectively writing off half the inventory held. Joshua has decided to reduce the write - down to 10% of the inventory value.

This decision was taken by Joshua just before his annual holiday and so he instructed Nadia to make the appropriate adjustments.

Identify and explain five weaknesses in the general ledger system and suggest an improvement for each weakness to reduce the risk of error or misstatement.   (15 marks)

Weakness	Suggestion for improvement

Weakness	Suggestion for improvement

Section 3

ANSWERS TO PRACTICE QUESTIONS

TASK 1.1

Assessment objective 1	Demonstrate an understanding of the roles and responsibilities of the accounting function within an organisation and examine ways of preventing and detecting fraud and systemic weaknesses.

1 STATUTORY DUTY

Who has the statutory duty to prepare accounts for Ruby Dale?

The company auditors.	
The directors of the company.	✓
Joshua Edeki, Finance Director.	
Erika Tordoff, Financial Controller.	
Companies House.	

2 RESPONSIBILITY

Who is responsible for maintaining sound risk management and internal control systems within Ruby Dale?

The company auditors.	
The directors of the company.	✓
Joshua Edeki, Finance Director.	
Erika Tordoff, Financial Controller.	
Companies House.	

3 BANK RECONCILIATION 1

Adjustment	Amount £	Debit/Credit
Adjustment for (2)	106	Cr
Adjustment for (3)	350	Dr
Adjustment for (4)	1,645	Dr

Note:

Reconciliation

Cash book

Balance b/d	103	ADJUSTMENT (2)	106
ADJUSTMENT (3)	350		
ADJUSTMENT (4)	1,645		
		Balance c/d	1,992
	2,098		2,098

Balance of bank account	363
Uncleared lodgements	1,629
	1,992

4   BANK RECONCILIATION 2

	Yes	No
A customer was accidentally invoiced twice for the same item.		✓
An independent retailer took a 2% prompt payment discount despite not having paid within the timescales required to earn a discount.		✓
Bank interest received had not been posted to the cash book.	✓	
A payment to a supplier of £2,500 had accidentally been posted as £250.	✓	

5   SALES LEDGER CONTROL ACCOUNT RECONCILIATION 1

	Add/Subtract	£
Total from list of balances		31,100
Adjustment for (a)	Add	65
Adjustment for (b)	Subtract	280
Adjustment for (c)	Subtract	1,170
Adjustment for (d)	Add	3,600
Adjustment for (e)	Subtract	99
Adjustment for (f)	Subtract	100
Revised total to agree with SLCA		33,116

6   SALES LEDGER CONTROL ACCOUNT RECONCILIATION 2

	Yes	No
A customer was accidentally invoiced twice for the same item.		✓
An independent retailer was sold items at the wrong price.		✓
Credit balances had been omitted from the list of receivables balances.	✓	
A payment from a customer of £230 had accidentally been posted as £320 to their individual account in the receivables ledger.	✓	

7   PURCHASES LEDGER CONTROL ACCOUNT RECONCILIATION

	Add/Subtract	£
Total from list of balances		132,589
Adjustment for (a)	Add	445
Adjustment for (b)	Subtract	4,340
Adjustment for (c)	Subtract	1,200
Adjustment for (d)	Subtract	132
Adjustment for (e)	Add	2,100
Adjustment for (f)	Add	120
Revised total to agree with PLCA		129,582

8   ERRORS

(a)   Journal

	Dr £	Cr £
Motor expenses	4,500	
Motor vehicles at cost		4,500

(b)   Journal

	Dr £	Cr £
Office sundries	16	
Suspense		16

(c)   Journal

	Dr £	Cr £
Closing inventory – statement of financial position	189,320	
Closing inventory – statement of profit or loss		189,320

Working

Inventory is valued at the lower of cost and net realisable value. The selling price is given as £227,184. To get to the selling price, 20% of the value of the cost is added to the cost. The cost of £189,320 has been calculated by dividing the selling price by 120 and then multiplying by 100. (227,184/120) × 100 = 189,320.

The value of closing inventory, in accordance with IAS 2 is £189,320.

(d)   Journal

	Dr £	Cr £
Receivables	1,720	
Discounts allowed		1,720
Discounts allowed	1,270	
Receivables		1,270

9   CHANGEOVER

Which TWO of the following controls can mitigate the risk of system failure during direct changeover?

Testing	✓
Training	
System documentation	
Data backup	✓
Check digits	

Note: Testing reduces the probability of failure, and data backup reduces the impact.

10 INFORMATION SYSTEM CONTROLS

	Security	Integrity
Locked doors	✓	
Passwords	✓	
Batch totals		✓
Reconciliation		✓
CCTV	✓	
Check digits		✓
Authorisation of data entry		✓
Fire alarms	✓	

11 PURCHASE CYCLE CONTROLS 1

Which TWO of the following controls in a purchase cycle could be implemented to reduce the risk of payment of goods not received?

Sequentially pre-numbered purchase requisitions and sequence check.	
Matching of goods received note with purchase invoice.	✓
Goods are inspected for condition and quantity and agreed to purchase order before acceptance.	✓
Daily update of inventory system.	

12 PURCHASE CYCLE CONTROLS 2

Which TWO of the following controls in the purchase cycle could be implemented to reduce the risk of procurement of unnecessary goods and services?

Centralised purchasing department.	✓
Sequentially pre-numbered purchase requisitions and sequence check.	
Orders can only be placed with suppliers from the approved suppliers list.	
All purchase requisitions are signed as authorised by an appropriate manager.	✓

13 EXPENSE CLAIM CONTROLS

Which ONE of the following essential internal control measures is evidently missing from Ruby Dale Ltd?

Ruby Dale lacks a control environment as the board are not setting an ethical tone at the top.	✓
Ruby Dale lacks an Internal Audit department.	
Ruby Dale lacks an experienced finance manager.	
Ruby Dale lacks an external auditor.	

14 PASSWORDS 1

Which of the following would be the most secure?

24june1963	
LaraJo	
mypassword	
Qwerty123!#	✓

15 PASSWORDS 2

Which TWO of the following would reduce the effectiveness of passwords?

Requirement that passwords are changed every two weeks	
Users are allowed to choose their own passwords	✓
Automatic lock-out after 3 failed attempts to access system	
Making the sharing of passwords a disciplinary offence	
Displaying the password on the screen when entered	✓

16 INTERNAL CONTROLS 1

Match each of the following activities to the component that it illustrates.

	Control environment	Information system	Control activities
The process of preparing the financial statements		✓	
Locking the inventory storeroom			✓

17 INTERNAL CONTROLS 2

Match each of the following activities to the type of control that it illustrates.

	Authorisation	Information processing	Physical control
The financial controller will count petty cash on a weekly basis			✓
There will be two keys to the locked safe: one held by the FD and the other by the MD.			✓

18   INTERNAL CONTROLS 3

Match each of the following activities to the type of computer control that it illustrates.

	General	Application
Storing extra copies of programs and data files off-site	✓	
New programmes to check data fields on input transactions		✓
Manual checks to ensure that input data were authorised		✓
Password protection limiting access to data	✓	
Range checks on payroll processing		✓
Manual checks to ensure that timesheets are authorised before details are processed		✓

19   INTERNAL CONTROLS 4

Indicate whether the following limitations are true or false.

	True	False
The cost of implementing controls may be more expensive than the benefits gained due to reduced risk	✓	
The effectiveness of many controls rely on the integrity of those applying them	✓	
Internal controls are only applied to material items		✓
Standard controls may not be designed to deal with unusual transactions	✓	

20   FRAUD 1

Which THREE of the following control activities would best prevent this fraud occurring?

Segregation of duties between cash handling and recording	✓
Post opening by two people	✓
Investigation of differences between website sales and cash banked	
Regular banking of cash and cheques received in the post	✓

21   FRAUD 2

Which ONE of the following control activities would best prevent this occurring?

Payroll standing data periodically printed out and checked on a line-by-line basis to independently held employee details	
Use of hierarchical passwords over standing data files	✓
Pre-authorisation of all amendments to payroll standing data by an independent official	
Supervision of the wages pay out by an independent official	

Note: In order to prevent this from happening, the key is that fictitious employees never make it onto the payroll.

- Printing out and checking standing data will detect any fictitious employees added but will not prevent them from being added.

- Use of hierarchical passwords over standing data files ensures that an unscrupulous employee cannot access the part of the system where new employees would be added and hence will prevent the fraud. This is therefore the correct answer.

- Pre-authorisation of all amendments will not prevent the addition as an unscrupulous employee will not ask for authorisation but will simply add the fictitious details if the system allows them to do this.

- Supervision of the wages pay out by an independent official might detect dummy employees but would be unlikely to prevent the fraud.

TASK 1.2

Assessment objective 2	Evaluate budgetary reporting; its effectiveness in controlling and improving organisational performance.

22   TRAINING COSTS

(a)   BRIEFLY discuss THREE weaknesses in the above use of performance reports to improve the focus of training within Ruby Dale.

Weakness 1
Flexing
The budget is a fixed one; meaning it has not been flexed for the 25% increase in activity.
A flexible budget is one where the turnover and variable costs are changed in line with the change in activity. In this case they would be increased by 25%. Fixed costs remain unchanged from the original budget.
The advantage of fixed budgeting is that it takes less time and is, therefore, less costly to produce; the disadvantage is that variances are less meaningful and, therefore, control is effectively reduced. The advantage and disadvantage of flexible budgeting are the opposite of this.
The flexed budget cost would be
$$13{,}000 + 1{,}000 \times (25/20) = £14{,}250$$
This gives an overall favourable variance of £150 rather than an adverse one of £100. The manager should thus be praised rather than reprimanded.

Weakness 2
Participation in target setting and budgeting
Petr Higgs was not involved in setting the original budget and did not even know about it. This lack of participation could easily result in him viewing the target as unfair and unrealistic, resulting in demotivation. It is also very difficult to be motivated to hit a target you are unaware of!
Greater participation will help resolve these issues and also may result in more realistic budgets in the first place. The main disadvantage of participation is the possibility of budget "padding", where Petr may have tried to set an easy target for himself.
Weakness 3
Emphasis on financial factors
The sole emphasis on financial factors only may result in Petr being more concerned about cost control than delivering high quality training.
The directors were concerned that training lacked focus rather than it being too expensive. There is nothing in the email to see if focus has improved.
Weakness 4
Mark Austin's tone
Mark Austin's tone is far too aggressive, particularly given the above factors, and is likely to result in resentment and demotivation.
This is particularly the case as it is the first month of the new system, so there is a significant possibility that budgeted figures are not representative in the first place. The variance could thus be due to planning errors rather than Petr's operational performance.

(b) Outline THREE performance indicators that could be used to assess the quality of the training provided.

Performance Indicator 1
Trainee feedback
Trainees could be asked to score different elements of the training process on a score of 1 to 5 say. This would indicate whether or not they felt the training was useful to them and would indicate areas for improvement.
Performance Indicator 2
Manager feedback
Presumably managers had objectives when sending staff on training courses/events – for example, to improve IT skills. Managers could be asked to assess whether they felt that their staff had benefited from the training – for example, were they more able to undertake required tasks in their roles? Again, a score of 1 to 5 would allow easier monitoring of feedback.
Performance Indicator 3
Objective scoring using tests
For some training – for example, awareness of company products – it may be possible to set a quiz or test before and after training to see if trainee's knowledge and awareness had improved.

(Total 15 marks)

23   BUDGETING

Evaluate the Ruby Dale budget for 20X6 by reference to the following assumed (or implied) growth rates and margins. In your answer discuss whether or not you feel the figures are realistic and why.   (15 marks)

Figure	Whether or not realistic
Sales volume growth of 10.0%	Growth of 10% in Asia seems reasonable, especially given the weakness of the pound, rising levels of disposable incomes and increasing brand awareness. Furthermore, Ruby Dale is planning to release five new lines of bags and has received a boost to its reputation by winning an industry award at the end of 20X5. In addition, the budgeted growth is less than the industry forecast of 12%, again suggesting the target is achievable.
Sales revenue growth of 8.0%	Compared to volume growth of 10%, sales growth of 8% seems even more reasonable. The difference would imply a fall in the average price, either due to a cut in prices or a change is sales mix. Either of these factors could be explained by increased competition but the weakening pound should mitigate the need for (or impact) of price cuts.
Cost of sales growth of 7.0%	Cost of sales growth of only 7% seems low compared to sales volume growth of 10%. One way of explaining this difference between would only be feasible if a significant proportion of cost of sales were fixed costs rather than variable. This seems likely as the main part of cost of sales will be the labour cost of cutting and stitching leather. Furthermore, the impact of outsourcing bag production may also bring cost savings.
Gross margin of 48.7%	If the above assumptions regarding growth hold to be valid, then the end result will be a gpm of 48.7%. Furthermore, the increase is only small compared to the actual figures achieved in 20X5.
Fall in selling costs of 1.3%	A significant proportion of selling and distribution costs can be expected to be variable, so it is questionable how Ruby Dale expects to see these costs fall by 1.3% when sales volume is increasing by 10%. One possibility is that distribution costs could fall for bags both sold and made within Asia due to shorter distances.
Fall in administration costs of 17.5%	Administration costs are likely to be mainly fixed in nature, so the only way such a large decrease can be achieved would be as a result of significant cost efficiencies. There is no information to suggest that such cost savings are feasible.

Conclusion – whether or not the budget is realistic

Overall the budget looks reasonable in terms of sales growth and cost behaviour, especially if plans to outsource bag product ion to Asia are fully implemented in time to impact the budget.

24   RUBY DALE BUDGETING PROCESS

Strengths

- Inflation should be allowed for as this leads to more accurate budgets

- Materials costs seem to be accounted for correctly

- Marketing seems to be based on only those products that the directors wish to specifically promote, reducing the possibility of cost overspends or unfocussed marketing expenditure

- Some attempt is made to account for the effectiveness of the marketing spend using regression analysis

Weaknesses

- Whilst choice over RPI and CPI is good for motivation it can lead to inconsistency and confusion for managers that are unaware of the difference and appropriateness of these.

- No inflationary guidance is given for costs other than wages, rents and materials implying that these other costs are "minor". This therefore excludes, for example, distribution costs, which are significant.

- Past inflation is not necessarily equal to future inflation – for example, after the Brexit vote in the UK, inflation jumped considerably compared to past measures

- Rent might not be affected by inflation at all. Leases have fixed rent review points and can sometimes be influenced by general market condition as well as inflation

- Other sales managers are not consulted on any local marketing need. This can be demotivating and might not address concerns over poor performance – for example, Jenni Black may feel that Ruby Dale needs to spend more promoting its online presence

- Past marketing to sales trends may not continue given the ever-changing markets

- Sales volumes change for other reasons (not just marketing)

Opportunities

- A central decision should be made regarding the inflation measure to be used

- More complete inflationary guidance could be given to include all costs lines

- Guidance could be given concerning rental budgets, suggesting that existing leases be reviewed for rent revision dates

- Greater account could be given to current market conditions when predicting sales (rather than relying purely on past regression)

Threats

- If inflation is under estimated on a cost then this could lead to an under budgeted costs and adverse variances. The opposite is true for overestimated inflation

- Omission of inflationary guidance for (in particular) cost of sales could lead to a significant budget error, loss of confidence in the process and under funding

- Sales levels may disappoint if no local considerations are made

- Assuming that the past will continue into the future is misguided and new opportunities may be missed or complacency could set in

- Budget sales levels could be incorrect leading to poor assumptions about profitability

TASK 1.3

Assessment objective 3	Evaluate an organisation's accounting control systems and procedures.

25   RUBY DALE'S PURCHASING SYSTEM

Required:

Identify and explain FOUR deficiencies in the system, explain the possible implication of each deficiency and provide a recommendation to address each deficiency. **(15 marks)**

Deficiency	Implication	Recommendation
When raising purchase orders, the clerks choose whichever supplier can dispatch the goods the fastest.	This could result in Ruby Dale ordering goods at a much higher price or a lower quality than they would like, as the only factor considered was speed of delivery. It is important that goods are dispatched promptly, but this is just one of many criteria that should be used in deciding which supplier to use.	An approved supplier list should be compiled; this should take into account the price of goods, their quality and also the speed of delivery. Once the list has been produced, all orders should only be placed with suppliers on the approved list.

Purchase orders are not sequentially numbered.	Failing to sequentially number the orders means that Ruby Dale's ordering team is unable to monitor if all orders are being fulfilled in a timely manner; this could result in stock outs. If the orders are numbered, then a sequence check can be performed for any unfulfilled orders.	All purchase orders should be sequentially numbered and on a regular basis a sequence check of unfulfilled orders should be performed.
Purchase orders below £1,000 are not authorised and are processed solely by an order clerk.	This can result in goods being purchased which are not required by Ruby Dale. In addition, there is an increased fraud risk as an order clerk could place orders for personal goods up to the value of £1,000, which is significant.	All purchase orders should be authorised by a responsible official. Authorised signatories should be established with varying levels of purchase order authorisation.
Purchase invoices are input daily by the purchase ledger clerk and due to his experience, he does not utilise any application controls.	Without application controls there is a risk that invoices could be input into the system with inaccuracies or they may be missed out entirely. This could result in suppliers being paid incorrectly or not all, leading to a loss of supplier goodwill.	The purchase ledger clerk should input the invoices in batches and apply application controls, such as control totals, to ensure completeness and accuracy over the input of purchase invoices.
The purchase day book automatically updates with the purchase ledger but this ledger is manually posted to the general ledger.	Manually posting the amounts to the general ledger increases the risk of errors occurring. This could result in the payables balance in the financial statements being under or overstated.	The process should be updated so that on a regular basis the purchase ledger automatically updates the general ledger. A responsible official should then confirm through purchase ledger control account reconciliations that the update has occurred correctly.

Ruby Dale's saving (deposit) bank accounts are only reconciled every two months.	If these accounts are only reconciled periodically, there is the risk that errors will not be spotted promptly. Also, this increases the risk of employees committing fraud. If they are aware that these accounts are not regularly reviewed, then they could use these cash sums fraudulently.	All bank accounts should be reconciled on a regular basis, and at least monthly, to identify any unusual or missing items. The reconciliations should be reviewed by a responsible official and they should evidence their review.
Ruby Dale has a policy of delaying payments to their suppliers for as long as possible.	Whilst this maximises Ruby Dale's bank balance, there is the risk that Ruby Dale is missing out on early settlement discounts. Also, this can lead to a loss of supplier goodwill as well as the risk that suppliers may refuse to supply goods to Ruby Dale.	Ruby Dale should undertake cash flow forecasting/ budgeting to maximise bank balances. The policy of delaying payment should be reviewed, and suppliers should be paid in a systematic way, such that supplier goodwill is not lost.

Note: only FOUR required.

26 RUBY DALE'S SALES AND INVENTORY PROCESSES

Required:

In respect of the internal control of Ruby Dale's sales and inventory processes, identify FIVE deficiencies, explain the possible implication of each deficiency and recommend a control to address each of these deficiencies. **(15 marks)**

Deficiency	Implication	Recommendation
Currently the website is not integrated into inventory system.	This can result in Ruby Dale accepting customer orders when they do not have the goods in inventory. This can cause them to lose sales and customer goodwill.	The website should be updated to include an interface into the inventory system; this should check inventory levels and only process orders if adequate inventory is held. If inventory is out of stock, this should appear on the website with an approximate waiting time.

For goods despatched by local couriers, customer signatures are not always obtained.	This can lead to customers falsely claiming that they have not received their goods. Ruby Dale would not be able to prove that they had in fact despatched the goods and may result in goods being despatched twice.	Ruby Dale should remind all local couriers that customer signatures must be obtained as proof of despatch and payment will not be made for any despatches with missing signatures.
There have been a number of situations where the sales orders have not been fulfilled in a timely manner.	This can lead to a loss of customer goodwill and if it persists will damage the reputation of Ruby Dale as a reliable supplier.	Once goods are despatched they should be matched to sales orders and flagged as fulfilled. The system should automatically flag any outstanding sales orders past a predetermined period, such as five days. This report should be reviewed by a responsible official.
Customer credit limits are set by sales ledger clerks.	Sales ledger clerks are not sufficiently senior and so may set limits too high, leading to irrecoverable debts, or too low, leading to a loss of sales.	Credit limits should be set by a senior member of the sales ledger department and not by sales ledger clerks. These limits should be regularly reviewed by a responsible official.
Sales discounts are set by Ruby Dale's sales team.	In order to boost their sales, members of the sales team may set the discounts too high, leading to a loss of revenue.	All members of the sales team should be given authority to grant sales discounts up to a set limit. Any sales discounts above these limits should be authorised by sales area managers or the sales director. Regular review of sales discount levels should be undertaken by the sales director, and this review should be evidenced.

Supplier statement reconciliations are no longer performed.	This may result in errors in the recording of purchases and payables not being identified in a timely manner.	Supplier statement reconciliations should be performed on a monthly basis for all suppliers and these should be reviewed by a responsible official.
Changes to supplier details in the purchase ledger master file can be undertaken by purchase ledger clerks.	This could lead to key supplier data being accidently amended or fictitious suppliers being set up, which can increase the risk of fraud.	Only purchase ledger supervisors should have the authority to make changes to master file data. This should be controlled via passwords. Regular review of any changes to master file data by a responsible official and this review should be evidenced.
Ruby Dale has considerable levels of surplus plant and equipment.	Surplus unused plant is at risk of theft. In addition, if the surplus plant is not disposed of then the company could lose sundry income.	Regular review of the plant and equipment on the factory floor by senior factory personnel to identify any old or surplus equipment. As part of the capital expenditure process there should be a requirement to confirm the treatment of the equipment being replaced.
Purchase requisitions are authorised by production supervisors.	Production supervisors are not sufficiently independent or senior to authorise capital expenditure.	Capital expenditure authorisation levels to be established. Production supervisors should only be able to authorise low value items, any high value items should be authorised by the board.

Note: only FIVE required.

27 RUBY DALE'S INVENTORY COUNTING PROCESSES

Weakness	Effect of Weakness
The internal auditor should attend as an observer only and not get involved in the count itself. To do so confuses the roles of the people involved.	Errors in process might not have been detected as the internal auditor was busy "doing" rather than "observing". It is also possible that the internal auditor who is not an employee is not competent to recognize damaged or slow moving inventory and so these items could go unrecorded.
Weakness	**Effect of Weakness**
The instructions are capable of misinterpretation. Staff seem to have been instructed to record all items that are shown on the sheets as being in a certain location. They might not record items that are therefore in the wrong location, or only look in designated locations rather than all possible places where inventory may be held.	This could lead to serious understatement of the inventory values and hence an understatement of profit.
The designation of duties is a little unclear. The two unallocated zones appear to fall between two counting teams and so the count is then dependent on the organisation of the spare resource on the count day.	An area could either be missed or be counted by both teams. This could lead to over or under statement of the inventory and hence profit.
The delivery that took place on the day of the count might not have been accounted for properly. It is not clear from the question what happened to the actual counting of the delivery. The items should have been included, even though they were in the car park at the time. Equally, details of the delivery should have been recorded so that correct cut off with regards to purchases could subsequently be checked.	The items could have been incorrectly excluded and so inventory understated. Without delivery details being recorded a cut off error could have occurred. Consistency between the recording of inventory and the recording of purchases is important and without this the incorrect profit will be calculated.
Box labelling was relied on for the contents of boxes. This is an unreliable method. Damaged items within the boxes would not be identified.	Inventory could be misstated as the content of the boxes might not reflect the labelling. If damaged items are not identified then the inventory will be overstated.
Old items (slow-moving) were not identified or recorded during the count.	The accounting policy cannot be checked against the actual figures and so Ruby Dale might not detect and error in that policy.

Note: only FIVE required.

TASK 1.4

Assessment objective 4	Analyse an organisation's decision making and control using management accounting tools.

28 PRODUCTION DECISIONS

(a) BRIEFLY discuss the validity of each of the three directors' views on how the final decision should be made as to which shoes to make. **(9 marks)**

Managing Director
The Managing Director is basing decisions on the reported profits of each product. The reported operating profits include an arbitrary allocation of fixed costs that undermines their credibility.
While the Managing Director is correct that fixed costs must be covered somewhere, they are irrelevant to the decision as they are by definition unavoidable regardless of the decision.
Decisions should be made on the basis of future incremental cash flows.

Sales Director
The Sales Director is basing decisions on the contribution of each product. This has the advantage of considering only the future relevant cash flows and ignoring the allocated fixed overheads.
Looking at total contribution would only be appropriate if there was enough space to stock sufficient shoes to meet full demand, which is not the case here.
Unit contribution would be appropriate if all shoes involved the same amount of skilled labour, but, again, this is not the case here.

Production Director
The Production Director has the best overall approach as he is considering contribution, thus looking at relevant cash flows and ignoring allocated overheads.
In addition, and unlike the Sales Director, he is then incorporating how much time is taken to make each shoe. The ranking based on contribution per unit of scarce resource (i.e. time) should ensure that the use of skilled labour is maximised to generate the most contribution possible.

(b) BRIEFLY explain THREE other factors should be taken into consideration before making a final decision. **(6 marks)**

Factor 1
How much labour is available
The decision is focussed on selecting just one shoe to stock. However, it may be that there is sufficient labour to make many ranges, even if there is not enough for all of them.
For example, making 400 Ds would need 400 × 110 = 44,000 minutes. This is sufficient for all of the Cs (requires 200 × 102 = 24,000) and a significant number of Bs, say.
Furthermore, it may be possible to increase the amount of available labour by asking staff to work overtime, although the overtime premium paid would have to be factored into the contribution calculations.

Factor 2
Whether customers are willing to wait
For some shoes, customers may be happy to order on the website and wait until the next production run of those models. If this is the case, then Ruby Dale could simply wait until they have a month with spare capacity and make these models then

Factor 3
The figures used
The decision has been based on the figures available. However, these may change, possibly affecting the decision.
For example, discounts have been ignored but if one shoe tends to attract more discounts, say to boost falling demand, then the price (and hence contribution per minute) would fall, changing the ranking.

29   NEW SUPPLIERS

(a) **Which of the following prices should be used for target costing?**   **(2 marks)**

The budgeted price that Ruby Dale has set for 20X6	✓
The existing price that Ruby Dale uses	
The market average price	
The price charged by Ruby Dale's main competitor for a similar game	

(b) **Calculate the target cost for a large satchel.**   **(3 marks)**

Cost per unit	£
Production cost (charged by supplier) = balancing figure	**97.62**
Transportation costs (given)	5.50
Total cost = 165 × 100/150	**103.12**
Mark up = 165 × 60/160	61.88
Target selling price	**165.00**

(c) **Briefly explain how the concept of value analysis applies to Ruby Dale and the options available to it to close any cost gap.**   **(4 marks)**

Value analysis
Value analysis involves considering which aspects of the product are valued by the customer.
This would allow Ruby Dale to identify possible areas for cutting costs to close any target cost 'gap' without compromising the value to the customer.
For Ruby Dale the ultimate consumer will value the designs, the quality of leather used, the quality of finish (e.g. stitching) and the brand, so these should not be compromised.
However, customers may be less concerned about the quality of packaging or the buckles, so cost savings may be possible here.

Options available to Ruby Dale
Ruby Dale may be able to reduce transportation costs by choosing suppliers who are closer to key markets, such as Asia.
Apart from this the only option is to get lower prices from suppliers, whether through cheaper materials or switching suppliers.
Obviously it must be careful not to compromise customer perceived quality when doing this.

(d) **Discuss which supplier should be chosen by referring to both financial and non-financial factors.** **(6 marks)**

Financial factors
Target cost
Both suppliers B and C meet the target cost criteria, with C being the cheapest.
However, A may meet the target cost depending on the extent of any bulk discount offered.
This may be significant as the satchel is one of Ruby Dale's most popular bag styles.
Non-financial factors
Quality of supply
The main problem with C is the long delivery time as this will either mean potential delays to customers or that mean that Ruby Dale will need to hold higher inventory levels. Delays to customers should be avoided given the importance of customer loyalty and satisfaction. On the other hand, holding more inventory will increase the length of the cash operating cycle. This may not be acceptable given fears regarding possible overtrading. Delivery times would favour A and B.
Linked to cash flow problems we can also look at credit terms. Longer credit terms take the pressure off Ruby Dale's cash cycle suggesting that B should be chosen
Quality of product
It is important that customers feel that they are buying a quality product that reflects the brand.
Supplier C's approach to stitching and buckles may be seen as inferior to the current offering, so could erode brand perception and loyalty, especially if this gets discussed on social media.
Supplier B seems to be matching the current product, whereas Supplier A is improving quality by using brass buckles. Unfortunately this may mean that the cost is too high resulting in Ruby Dale failing to hit the mark-up required. It is also debatable whether customers would value brass buckles unless the bag is advertised as a premium range.

30   RUBY DALE PORTFOLIO PLANNING

(a)   Data table:

Quarter Number	Volume Units	Revenue £	Variable Cost £	Contribution £
1 (Q2 2017)	350	87,500	35,000	52,500
2 (Q3 2017)	290	72,500	29,000	43,500
3 (Q4 2017)	266	66,500	26,600	39,900
4 (Q1 2018)	258	64,500	25,800	38,700
5 (Q2 2018)	246	61,500	24,600	36,900
6 (Q3 2018)	238	59,500	23,800	35,700
7 (Q4 2018)	205	51,250	20,500	30,750
8 (Q1 2019)	185	46,250	18,500	27,750
9 (Q2 2019)	165	41,250	16,500	24,750
10 (Q3 2019)	145	36,250	14,500	21,750

(b)   Discussion of findings:

The value 'b'

The value b is the slope of the regression line, indicating by how much the value y declines (in this case) and the x value increases by 1 (1 quarter in this case). Hence it shows the decline in sales volume as time ticks by one quarter at a time. This is based on the average of past declines and there is no guarantee that past trend reflects the future. The decline could be greater or lower than the 20 pairs given.

Data findings

The data shows that this product's revenue will fall to £36,250 by the end of the planning horizon (Q3 2019). Over the same period the contribution gained also gradually falls and reaches only £21,750 by that same point.

The important point is that Ruby Dale will continue to make a positive contribution up to that quarter and so should be willing to continue to supply the product.

The data also states that this product's share of fixed costs are £25,000 and this might imply to some that cessation of supply is justified as the shoes will be loss making. However, it must be borne in mind that these fixed costs will not be avoidable on cessation and as such are not relevant to a cessation decision. If they were directly attributable, then they would be relevant.

Furthermore, the data only relates to sales on shoes of that range and does not include sales of matching bags and other linked products.

*(Note: do not make the mistake of thinking that the **actual** sales figures for quarters 1 to 6 should fit the regression line exactly. They do not! The equation is effectively an average – a line of best fit – of the historic results that can be used to predict the future)*

(c)   Non-financial considerations

> Businesses should not make all decisions purely based on the financial figures and this case is no different. The following considerations are worthy of note:
>
> Impact on customers – customers that own other shoes or bags worn by that celebrity in that particular may feel abandoned if they can no longer source new shoes
>
> Impact on staff staff – some staff may specialise in making the particular range concerned and so may face the need to retrain if the range is discontinued. On the other hand Ruby Dale has had capacity constraints so freeing up labour here could enable stock-outs elsewhere to be avoided

TASK 1.5

AO5	Analyse an organisation's decision making and control using ratio analysis.

31   RUBY DALE AND OVERTRADING

(a)   **Complete the scorecard by calculating the missing ratios.**   **(10 marks)**

RUBY DALE Scorecard	Y/e 30/9/X6	Y/e 30/9/X5
Profitability and gearing		
Gross profit %	58.4%	62.7%
Operating profit %	16.6%	**17.8%**
Return on capital employed	11.8%	**12.9%**
Gearing (debt/equity)	0.65×	0.55×
Liquidity ratios		
Current ratio	2.8:1	2.2:1
Acid test/Quick ratio	2.4:1	**1.3:1**
Working capital days		
Inventory holding period	75 days	**89 days**
Trade receivables collection period	71 days	67 days
Trade payables payment period	60 days	74 days
Working capital cycle	86 days	**57 days**

Workings

- Operating profit margin = (7,358/41,380) × 100% = 17.8%

- ROCE = [7,358/(36,836 + 20,286)] × 100% = 12.9%

- Quick ratio = (676 + 4,762)/4,276 = 1.3:1

- Inventory days = (3,780/15,434) × 365= 89 days

- Working capital cycle = 89 + 42 – 74 = 57 days

(b) **Select the ONE correct observation about each aspect of business performance below.** **(10 marks)**

Profitability

20X6 will be a year of steady, if unspectacular, progress. Although margins have dipped, the return on capital employed has been kept constant.	
The changes in gross margin could be due to cost control problems concerning distribution.	
Increased competition and the resulting pressure on prices could explain the change in each of the three profitability ratios.	✓

Gearing

The increased gearing ratio proves that RUBY DALE has no problems raising additional debt finance.	
It is likely that the interest cover ratio has increased.	
The increased gearing ratio shows that the shareholders' position has become more risky.	✓

Liquidity

Both ratios have increased, which indicates that the company is less solvent.	
A higher quick ratio is a clear indicator of overtrading.	
The change in both the current and quick ratios could be partly explained by the increase in the receivables period.	✓

Working capital

The working capital cycle has worsened. This increases the possibility of RUBY DALE overtrading.	✓
There is a welcome improvement in the working capital cycle, mainly due to the change in the payment period for payables.	
The working capital cycle is worse than a year ago because of the change in inventory days.	

Overall performance

Despite overall growth, RUBY DALE is having a difficult year in 20X6 and needs to investigate why key ratios are deteriorating.	✓
20X6 looks to be a disaster for RUBY DALE.	
There is no evidence of possible control problems.	

32 RUBY DALE – COMPETITOR ANALYSIS

(a) Complete the scorecard by calculating the missing ratios. (10 marks)

Y/e 30/09/X5	Ruby Dale	Rival
Profitability		
Gross profit %	62.7%	**49.3%**
Operating profit %	17.8%	9.5%
Return on capital employed	12.9%	**27.9%**
Liquidity ratios		
Current ratio	2.2:1	**2.0:1**
Acid test/Quick ratio	1.3:1	0.6:1
Working capital days		
Inventory holding period	89 days	60 days
Trade receivables collection period	42 days	32 days
Trade payables payment period	74 days	**30 days**
Working capital cycle	57 days	**62 days**

(b) Assess the following statements concerning potential control problems and indicate whether they are true or false. (10 marks)

Statement	True	False
The difference in gross margins could be explained by the Rival giving excessive discounts in "sales" to shift excess inventory.	✓	
If Ruby Dale has delayed paying suppliers at the year end, then this would contribute to the difference in current ratios.		✓
The difference in the lengths of the working capital cycles could be explained by a credit controller at Ruby Dale being off work due to illness.		✓
A warehouse employee in Ruby Dale was found to have stolen bags and sold them on an online auction site. This would contribute to the difference in the ROCE figures.	✓	
Inadequate controls over expense claims for managers within Ruby Dale could contribute to the difference in the operating margins figures.	✓	

33 CASH AND PROFIT

Why is profit important in business? (5 marks)

Profits are the generally accepted measure of the successful trading of a business.

Profit is the most commonly used measure of performance with analysts looking at figures for profit, profit margins and return on capital employed. As such the determination of profit is heavily regulated.

This regulation (in the form of standard accounting practices) ensures that all companies measure profit is broadly the same way and in this way, it is trusted by investors and management to reflect performance.

The press often focusses on profitability when commenting on a business's performance and this tends to increase the profile of the profit measure on all concerned.

Why must cash also be considered in business? (5 marks)

Cash in this context is the cash balance of the business at any one time and also the amount of cash the business has generated or spent over the accounting period.

Cash is seen as vital in business for a number of reasons:

Cash is used for investment. If a business wants to buy assets in order to grow, then it needs cash to do that. It can borrow that money, that is true, but in this case it will need cash to make the repayments on any loan it takes out.

Cash is also used to make normal commercial payments. Wages, suppliers, and stationery, all must be paid for with cash and so without cash these payments cannot be made and trade would stop.

The government also have a stake in businesses and although the regulation insists that profits are measured the government requires that corporate tax is paid. Although the amount of tax is in part determined by the profits made the company needs cash to actually make the payment.

Cash might also be needed for emergencies, to cover for example unexpected payments. Businesses often hold reserves of cash for this purpose.

Does the cash equal the profit? (5 marks)

In some ways, what Mark says is true. If he buys materials from a supplier then that will have to be paid for with cash. However, one important difference here is the timing of the purchase compared to the payment. There is often a lag between the purchase and the subsequent payment. Consequently although the two figures are the same they will be recorded at different points of time.

Also, there are other cash transactions that are not reflected in the profits of the business immediately. For example, when a business buys a piece of plant the cash outflow would be immediate and in total. The expense in the profit and loss account would slowly catch up over a number of years as depreciation is charged over the assets useful economic life but there would be a significant delay in the case of long existing assets.

The final major difference created between cash and profits is dividend. Dividend is a cash outflow but does not go through the profit and loss account at all.

For all the above reasons the amount a business has in cash is not equal to the profitability of the same business. In extreme cases, companies can be guilty of 'over-trading' – trying to grow too quickly and run out of cash despite being profitable.

> **Discuss whether delaying the rent payment will be effective in increasing profits and the ethical stance the accounting department should take to the request.** **(5 marks)**
>
> The accounts of a business are produced using generally accepted accounting principles. One of these is matching. The principle is that over an accounting period expense are related to that period regardless of the cash transactions.
>
> What this means is that if a rent payment is delayed (as is being suggested in this case) then it would still be necessary to reflect the full rent cost in the profit and loss account and an accrual entry would be made to record it.
>
> Consequently, delaying the rent payment would not be effective in increasing profits.
>
> Ethically the account staff will be bound by an ethical code and would therefore be expected to behave professionally and with due care. Where it is being suggested that an accounting error be deliberately made in order to manipulate the accounts then the accountants would have to resist and in some way refuse to make the adjustment.

TASK 1.6

Assessment objective 6	Analyse the internal controls of an organisation and make recommendations.

34   RUBY DALE'S INVENTORY STOCK TAKE

For the inventory count arrangements of Ruby Dale identify and explain FIVE deficiencies; and provide a recommendation to address each deficiency. **(15 marks)**

Deficiency	Recommendation
The warehouse manager is planning to supervise the inventory count. Whilst he is familiar with the inventory, he has overall responsibility for the inventory and so is not independent. He may want to hide inefficiencies and any issues that arise so that his department is not criticised.	An alternative supervisor who is not normally involved with the inventory, such as an internal audit manager, should supervise the inventory count. The warehouse manager and his team should not be involved in the count at all.
There are five teams of counters, each team having two members of staff. However, there is no clear division of responsibilities within the team. Therefore, both members of staff could count together rather than checking each other's count; and errors in their count may not be identified.	Each team should be informed that both members are required to count their assigned inventory separately. Therefore, one counts and the second member checks that the inventory has been counted correctly.
The internal audit teams are undertaking inventory counts rather than reviewing the controls and performing sample test counts. Their role should be focused on confirming the accuracy of the inventory counting procedures.	The internal audit counters should sample check the counting undertaken by the ten teams to provide an extra control over the completeness and accuracy of the count.

Deficiency	Recommendation
Once areas are counted, the teams are not flagging the aisles as completed. Therefore there is the risk that some areas of the warehouse could be double counted or missed out.	All aisles should be flagged as completed, once the inventory has been counted. In addition, internal audit or the count supervisor should check at the end of the count that all 20 aisles have been flagged as completed.
Inventory not listed on the sheets is to be entered onto separate sheets, which are not sequentially numbered. Therefore the supervisor will be unable to ensure the completeness of all inventory sheets.	Each team should be given a blank sheet for entering any inventory count which is not on their sheets. This blank sheet should be sequentially numbered, any unused sheets should be returned at the end of the count, and the supervisor should check the sequence of all sheets at the end of the count.
The sheets are completed in ink and are sequentially numbered, however, there is no indication that they are signed by the counting team. Therefore if any issues arise with the counting in an aisle, it will be difficult to follow up as the identity of the counting team will not be known.	All inventory sheets should be signed by the relevant team upon completion of an aisle. When the sheets are returned, the supervisor should check that they have been signed.
Damaged or obsolete items are not being stored in a central area, and instead the counter is just noting on the inventory sheets the level of damage or indicating obsolescence. However, it will be difficult for the finance team to decide on an appropriate level of write down if they are not able to see the damaged goods. In addition, if these goods are left in the aisles, they could be inadvertently sold to customers or moved to another aisle.	Damaged goods should be clearly flagged by the counting teams and moved to a central location. This will avoid the risk of selling these goods. A senior member of the finance team should then inspect these goods to assess the level of any write down or allowance.
The 30 September is a working day, so there will be movements of goods during the count. Inventory records could be under/overstated if goods are missed or double counted due to movements in the warehouse.	It may not be practical to stop all inventory movements as the business needs to continue. Any goods received from suppliers should be stored in one location and counted once at the end and included as part of raw materials. Goods to be despatched to customers should be kept to a minimum for the day of the count. It may make more sense to do the inventory check the next day on a Sunday.

Note: only FIVE required

35 RUBY DALE'S SALES AND DESPATCH SYSTEM

Identify and explain FIVE deficiencies in RUBY DALE's sales and despatch system and provide a recommendation to address each of these deficiencies. **(15 marks)**

Deficiency	Recommendation
Inventory availability for telephone orders is not checked at the time the order is placed. The order clerks manually check the availability later and only then inform customers if there is insufficient inventory available. There is the risk that where goods are not available, order clerks could forget to contact the customers, leading to unfulfilled orders. This could lead to customer dissatisfaction, and would impact RUBY DALE's reputation.	When telephone orders are placed, the order clerk should check the inventory system whilst the customer is on the phone; they can then give an accurate assessment of the availability of goods and there is no risk of forgetting to inform customers.
Telephone orders are not recorded immediately on the three part pre-printed order forms; these are completed after the telephone call. There is a risk that incorrect or insufficient details may be recorded by the clerk and this could result in incorrect orders being despatched or orders failing to be despatched at all, resulting in a loss of customer goodwill.	All telephone orders should be recorded immediately on the three part pre-printed order forms. The clerk should also double check all the details taken with the customer over the telephone to ensure the accuracy of the order recorded.
Telephone orders are not sequentially numbered. Therefore if orders are misplaced whilst in transit to the despatch department, these orders will not be fulfilled, resulting in dissatisfied customers.	The three part pre-printed orders forms should be sequentially numbered and on a regular basis the despatch department should run a sequence check of orders received. Where there are gaps in the sequence, they should be investigated to identify any missing orders.
Customers are able to place online orders which will exceed their agreed credit limit by 10%. This increases the risk of accepting orders from bad credit risks.	Customer credit limits should be reviewed more regularly by a responsible official and should reflect the current spending pattern of customers. If some customers have increased the level of their purchases and are making payments on time, then these customers' credit limits could be increased. The online ordering system should be amended to not allow any orders to be processed which will exceed the customer's credit limit.

Deficiency	Recommendation
A daily pick list is used by the despatch department when sending out customer orders. However, it does not appear that the goods are checked back to the original order; this could result in incorrect goods being sent out.	In addition to the pick list, copies of all the related orders should be printed on a daily basis. When the goods have been picked ready to be despatched, they should be cross checked back to the original order. They should check correct quantities and product descriptions, as well as checking the quality of goods being despatched to ensure they are not damaged.
Additional staff have been drafted in to help the two sales clerks produce the sales invoices. As the extra staff will not be as experienced as the sales clerks, there is an increased risk of mistakes being made in the sales invoices. This could result in customers being under or overcharged.	Only the sales clerks should be able to raise sales invoices. As RUBY DALE is expanding, consideration should be given to recruiting and training more permanent sales clerks who can produce sales invoices.
Discounts given to customers are manually entered onto the sales invoices by sales clerks. This could result in unauthorised sales discounts being given as there does not seem to be any authorisation required. In addition, a clerk could forget to manually enter the discount or enter an incorrect level of discount for a customer, leading to the sales invoice being overstated and a loss of customer goodwill.	For customers who are due to receive a discount, the authorised discount levels should be updated to the customer master file. When the sales invoices for these customers are raised, their discounts should automatically appear on the invoice. The invoicing system should be amended to prevent sales clerks from being able to manually enter sales discounts onto invoices.

Note: only FIVE required

36   RUBY DALE'S GENERAL LEDGER SYSTEM

Weakness	Suggestion for improvement
There appears to be no approval required for any journal entries made by Erika (or for that matter Nadia). This means that errors made in journals are much less likely to be discovered before the entry is made.	Journal suggestions should be formally drafted with reasons for them and approval sought. This approval should be indicated by a signature and the journal documentation filed.
Access to the general ledger is given to under-qualified staff. Nadia is the sales director making it unlikely that she holds an accounting qualification. Specifically, it is unlikely that the change to the provision for slow moving inventory could made correctly by someone without a thorough grasp of accounting rules. Errors could be made, deliberate or otherwise, in a crucial accounting document.	Access to the general ledger should be restricted to the FD and the CA only and this access should require password entry. Passwords should be a secret, changed regularly and sufficiently complicated to prevent guesswork being successful.
General ledger accounts can be created without authorisation. Dubious transactions could be hidden more easily in accounts created for the purpose.	The creation of general ledger accounts should only be possible by either the FD or the CA. In all cases when a general ledger account is created then the system should alert both the FD and CA that this has happened.
A change to accounting policy has been made without approval or indeed consultation. Accounting policies must be consistently applied and appropriate for the business. If changed then adjustments may be required in comparative figures and an explanation made in the financial statements	The board must approve changes to the accounting policy. Evidence for the need of such a change must be shown and the financial effect calculated.
The friendship between the FD and the CA could undermine the controls within the business. There is evidence of this already as the FD is not asking for sight of journals from the CA due to a "trusting" environment that exists between them.	The business would struggle to enforce a more business-like relationship at this stage (the friendship having been formed), consequently a third person should review all journals and jointly produced work. This might have to be an internal auditor or other person with the requisite accounting knowledge.

Section 4

MOCK ASSESSMENT QUESTIONS

TASK 1 (20 marks)

(a) As well as selling via independent retailers and its website, Ruby Dale also has shops in Manchester, London, Paris and New York. The general accounts clerk, Alfred Tait, visits the UK shops at random without prior notification and does spot checks on the tills at the shop. He counts the cash in the till, adjusts for the initial float and reconciles this figure to the record of sales made from the till system that day.

Which of the following activities would be revealed by such a control? One mark for each correct answer. (4 marks)

Forged bank notes had been accepted by the shop	Would be/ Would not be
A discount had been allowed for damaged packaging and so the sale had not been made at full price	Would be/ Would not be
Cash had been taken from the till to pay for a staff member's car parking	Would be/ Would not be
A customer had not paid the full amount promising to come back later	Would be/ Would not be

(b) Ruby Dale's New York shop has been underperforming and so the manager felt under pressure to improve performance. Having tried more legitimate tactics, in some desperation, he began to re-package customer returns with quality issues and to sell them as new versions. This meant his revenue was higher and his shop showed a higher gross profit %. (4 marks)

Which of the fundamental principles of ethical behaviour does this most threaten?

Confidentiality	
Professional behaviour and integrity	
Professional competence and due care	

What action should be taken? Tick all that apply.

The manager should be reminded of the ethical principles upon which the Ruby Dale business is built	
The manager should be fired for gross misconduct immediately	
Customers affected should be contacted and replacement shoes or bags provided	

(c)   Ruby Dale has been having problems with staff members using their own names as passwords and so it has decided to introduce new protocols for the password system.

To maintain the best control which of the following protocols should be introduced?

(2 marks)

All passwords must contain a capital letter	
All passwords must contain a number	
All passwords must be changed every quarter	
All of the above	

(d)   Alfred Tait, the general accounts clerk, maintains a non-current asset register which records all assets owned, their cost and depreciation and is reconciled in total and by category to the general ledger balances each year. The register is used to calculate depreciation with the total amount then being transferred to the general ledger.

Which of the following errors would be revealed by the existence of the register and its year end reconciliation?   (4 marks)

A machine was bought during the year and was entered as plant in the general ledger. The non-current assets register recorded this asset as a fixture and fitting.	Would be/ Not be
Depreciation on the above asset was applied at the rate of 15% rather than the correct 20%.	Would be/ Not be
An asset was stolen during the year but this theft was not discovered until well after the year end.	Would be/ Not be
An asset was bought during the year which included a substantial charge for delivery. The delivery charge was debited to distribution costs in the general ledger but as part of the asset cost in the non-current asset register	Would be/ Not be

(e)   The employee involved in the above asset theft was eventually caught whilst trying to steal again (this time inventory), which he intended to sell at the local market. It is suspected that these thefts had become habitual and that the he had a market stall selling stolen shoes and bags most weeks.   (4 marks)

Which of the fundamental principles of ethical behaviour does this most threaten?

(2 marks)

Confidentiality	
Professional behaviour and integrity	
Professional competence and due care	

What action should be taken? Tick all that apply.   (2 marks)

The employee should sacked for gross misconduct	
The employee should be sent a written warning over his conduct	
The employee should verbally be reminded of his obligations and warned against further indiscretions	

(f)   Entry to the non-current asset register is protected by a password.

Which of the following passwords is the most secure?   **(2 marks)**

Register!	
Hutton	
123456	
Gnd5dge	

TASK 2   **(15 marks)**

Ruby Dale sets a budget each year for the factory costs. The directors feel that consistency is important and so they adopt a top down approach. The production director, Mark Austin, along with other members of the senior management team, bases the budgets on past performance, an analysis of the general market conditions and the need of the business to grow and hence satisfy its owners. Once these budgets have been drafted they are sent to the individual managers within the factory and broken down into even monthly amounts to give monthly targets.

The factory is organised into different production lines making different shoes and bags. Each manager is responsible for the total costs of their production line, including apportioned overall factory overheads.

The remuneration of managers is as follows:

- Each manager earns a salary commensurate with the size of the production line managed, the number of staff they supervise and their experience to date.

- A bonus is possible if monthly costs incurred are less than that shown in the budget.

The managers are unhappy with this situation.

(a)   **Briefly explain why you think that the managers might be unhappy with the budget and rewards process outlined above.**   **(6 marks)**

Some of the managers are suggesting that the budgets be revised to take account of conditions that did not exist at the time of the original budget process being undertaken. Specifically the warehouse has experienced significant increases in business rates (a local tax) levied on them by the local council. Other managers have had to pay overtime to staff to cope with staff sickness.

(b) Explain the general principles involved in the decision to revise a budget and then briefly discuss whether you would recommend a budget revision be granted in the above specific situations.

(9 marks)

General principles

Business rates increases

Overtime

TASK 3   (15 marks)

Ruby Dale does not have an IT director or even an IT manager, instead the finance director, Joshua Edeki, has looked after the IT infrastructure and it seems to run well.

Space in the head office is limited and Joshua likes to keep an eye on things, consequently the main server is located in his office. This way, he reasons, no one can interfere with it without him seeing them.

The server is quite new and has the capacity to cope with expansion for a few years yet. It was quite expensive and of a good standard and that meant money was saved in avoiding the need for any back up machines or contract for the same. Data is backed up nightly using a Grandfather, Father, Son methodology. This means that three versions (generations) of the data is held at any one time.

Password setting is left up to the staff. Joshua had a bad experience at his last employer when his boss forgot his password and it took a week to effectively hack into the system. "Passwords have to be memorable, since just like a house if you lose your key you can't get in" is his motto. The staff like this approach and chose names of their children or even their own names as passwords. This system is built on trust and the staff are expected not to disclose their passwords to third parties or other staff members.

The accounts payable system is a fairly standard one. Suppliers have an account, which is created by Ella Mags (the accounts payable clerk) and payments are made on approved invoices monthly. Occasionally invoices go 'missing' and so Ella processes copies sent by the supplier directly to her. If key suppliers refuse to supply (as they haven't been paid) then this can disrupt the supply chain and cause delays.

The sales side is centrally processed from orders sent by all the independent shops, which are collated together in batches of 20 shops and processed together. Luke Sinclair (the accounts receivable clerk), checks that the batch header showing 20 shops (the size of the batch) ties in to the total after processing.

Use the answer spaces overleaf as follows:

- **Identify and explain five weaknesses from the above system description**

- **For each weakness briefly explain the effect it could have on the company**

Weakness	Effect of Weakness

TASK 4   (15 marks)

Due to market pressures, the Board of Ruby Dale are considering moving the existing factory to a larger (and cheaper) location outside of Manchester.

One possible location is under consideration. A staff member of Ruby Dale has considered the costs involved in a factory move but you have been asked to consider the approach and report back.

The staff member has produced the following schedule showing the various costs involved in the move:

Item	Notes	Cost included in the project appraisal
Research costs	Cost incurred to date in researching the existing and new cost structures of the two factories in question.	This has cost £2,000 to date including a valuation fee and director's time.
Rent	The existing factory is rented for £120,000 per annum. The lease comes to an end shortly and Ruby Dale will be able to exit.	This rent will be saved.
Staff costs	Existing Ruby Dale staff will be able to either move location to the new shop or take early retirement. Overall staff levels will fall by 20%	Those staff re-locating will cost £850,000 in employment costs. 20% of the £850,000 has been deducted as well.
Plant and equipment	The old production lines will not be transferred, as the new factory is larger and new lines would be more efficient. The new equipment will cost £800,000 and will have a useful economic life of 5 years.	Depreciation on old equipment will be saved of £40,000 per annum. £160,000 of extra depreciation per annum has been included for the new equipment.
Central allocated overhead	The new factory will be allocated with more overhead (as it is larger)	Allocated overhead will be £120,000 per annum for the new factory

You have been asked to review this analysis using the principles of relevant costing to help ensure that the correct decision is made.

Use the answer spaces overleaf as follows:

- Briefly explain the principles behind relevant cash flows for decision making.   (3 marks)

- Comment on each of the costs above as to whether the costs included in the appraisal are correct.   (10 marks)

- Suggest ONE cash flow type not included in the above table that should be considered in the project appraisal.   (2 marks)

(15 marks)

Relevant cash flow principles

Item	Comment on treatment
Research costs	
Rent	
Staff costs	

Item	Comment on treatment
Equipment	
Central allocated overhead	

Cash flows incorrectly excluded	
1	

TASK 5 (20 marks)

Ruby Dale uses performance measures in four areas or perspectives. These are shown in the background information but broadly are:

Perspective 1: Learning and training

Perspective 2: Internal business processes

Perspective 3: Customers

Perspective 4: Financial outlook

Data from the management information system is now provided, comparing the latest forecasts for 20X6 with actual figures for 20X5:

	Notes	20X6	20X5
Learning and training			
Staff retention rate		75%	85%
% Of staff on an apprenticeship		10%	15%
% Of staff attending service training		65%	75%
Staff wellbeing rating (out of 100)	1	55%	80%
Internal business processes			
Product returns rate – from shops		2%	2%
Product returns rate – from website sales		5%	5%
Customers			
Satisfaction of product			
– Items bought via shops	2	98%	98%
– Items bought through website	2	88%	90%
Website sales			
– Number of sales made		925,000	800,000
– Complaints about late delivery		4,300	4,000
– Complaints about incorrect goods delivered		3,100	2,000
Brand recognition	3	82%	85%
Financial outlook			
Gross profit%		63.2%	?%
Operating profit %		17.5%	?%
Inventory holding period		90 days	? days
Gearing (debt/total long term finance)	4	45.0%	?%

Notes:

1 This is assessed using a confidential staff questionnaire. The rating is a weighted index based on a variety of factors including the degree staff feel 'supported' and 'valued'.

2 This is assessed by customer survey.

3 This is assessed by external research.

4 Gearing is measured as debt/(debt + equity).

(a) **Complete the financial ratio calculations missing from the table (to one decimal place only)** **(4 marks)**

Financial outlook	Notes	20X6	20X5
Gross profit%		61.2%	
Operating profit %		16.1.0%	
Inventory holding period		90 days	
Gearing		45.0%	

(b) **With regard to complaints, which of the following statements is true?** **(2 marks)**

The rate of complaints is up in all categories	
Delivering on time is more important than delivering the right goods	
The overall complaint rate is up 0.05%	

(c) **Provide an interpretation of the performance of the business with regard to 'learning and training', clearly explaining the consequences for the business as a result of the data. Also explain at TWO links between the data in the learning and training perspective with one other category of performance assessment within the balanced scorecard.** **(14 marks)**

TASK 6   **(15 marks)**

Ruby Dale's payroll system and overtime

Permanent employees in both the factory and the warehouse work a standard number of hours per week as specified in their employment contract. However, when the factory (or the warehouse) is busy, staff can be requested by management to work overtime. This can either be paid on a monthly basis or accrued and taken as days off.

Employees record any overtime worked and days taken off on weekly overtime sheets which are sent to the payroll department. The standard hours per employee are automatically set up in the system and the overtime sheets are entered by clerks into the payroll package, which automatically calculates the gross and net pay along with relevant deductions. These calculations are not checked at all. Wages are increased by the rate of inflation each year and the clerks are responsible for updating the standing data in the payroll system.

Employees are paid on a monthly basis by bank transfer for their contracted weekly hours and for any overtime worked in the previous month. If employees choose to be paid for overtime, authorisation is required by production or warehouse managers of any overtime in excess of 30% of standard hours. If employees choose instead to take days off, the payroll clerks should check back to the 'overtime worked' report; however, this report is not always checked.

The 'overtime worked' report, which details any overtime recorded by employees, is run by the payroll department weekly and emailed to department heads for authorisation. The payroll department asks department heads to only report if there are any errors recorded. Department heads are required to arrange for overtime sheets to be authorised by an alternative responsible official if they are away on annual leave; however, there are instances where this arrangement has not occurred.

The payroll package produces a list of payments per employee; this links into the bank system to produce a list of automatic payments. The finance director reviews the total list of bank transfers and compares this to the total amount to be paid per the payroll records; if any issues arise then the automatic bank transfer can be manually changed by the finance director.

Required:

In respect of the payroll system of Ruby Dale, identify and explain FIVE deficiencies and recommend a control to address each of these deficiencies.

Deficiencies	Controls

Deficiencies	Controls

Deficiencies	Controls

Section 5

ANSWERS TO MOCK ASSESSMENT QUESTIONS

TASK 1

(a) **Which of the following activities would be revealed by such a control?**

Forged bank notes had been accepted by a shop	Would be
A discount had been allowed for damaged packaging and so the sale had not been made at full price	Would not be
Cash had been taken from the till to pay for a staff member's car parking	Would be
A customer had not paid the full amount promising to come back later	Would be

(b) **Which of the fundamental principles of ethical behaviour does this most threaten?**

Confidentiality	
Professional behaviour and integrity	✓
Professional competence and due care *There is no suggestion he doesn't know what he is doing!*	

What action should be taken? Tick all that apply.

The manager should be reminded of the ethical principles upon which the GPL business is built	✓
The manager should be fired for gross misconduct immediately *The manager cannot be dismissed immediately without following due process.*	
Customers affected should be contacted and replacement shoes or bags provided *If possible customers should be compensated if they received inferior goods*	✓

(c) **To maintain the best control which of the following protocols should be introduced?**

All passwords must contain a capital letter	
All passwords must contain a number	
All passwords must be changed every quarter	
All of the above	✓

(d)

A machine was bought during the year and was entered as plant in the general ledger. The non-current assets register recorded this asset as a fixture and fitting.	Would be: The reconciliation is by category
Depreciation on the above asset was applied at the rate of 15% rather than the correct 20%.	Would be: Given the detection above
An asset was stolen during the year but this theft was not discovered until well after the year end.	Would not be: Not at the year-end in any case
An asset was bought during the year which included a substantial charge for delivery. The delivery charge was debited to distribution costs in the general ledger but as part of the asset cost in the non-current asset register	Would be due to difference in total costs.

(e) **Which of the fundamental principles of ethical behaviour does this most threaten?**

Confidentiality	
Professional behaviour and integrity	✓
Professional competence and due care	

What action should be taken? Tick all that apply. **(2 marks)**

The employee should sacked for gross misconduct	✓
The employee should be sent a written warning over his conduct	
The employee should verbally be reminded of his obligations and warned against further indiscretions	

This is a serious offence warranting a gross misconduct dismissal

(f)

Register!	
Hutton	
123456	
Gnd5dge	✓

Generally, the more complicated the better, avoiding words, names and strings of any sort.

TASK 2

(a) | **Reasons for discontent could be as follows:**

No consultation. The managers may feel that they should be consulted about the level of budget set. These people are expected to manage their business areas but seem to be disregarded in the budget process

Level of difficulty of targets. It could be that the budget process has resulted in some difficult-to-achieve figures. If the targets are too difficult, then this could be de-motivating and indeed annoying, given that at least part of a manager's reward is based on the difference between actual figures and the budget.

Growth is presumed. Despite historic and expected future growth, customer taste and fashion can change quite rapidly, so sales of some lines may decline rather than grow through no fault of the production managers concerned.

Seasonal aspects seem to be ignored. The budget process simply splits the annual budget into equal monthly targets. Given Ruby Dale makes shoes and bags, it is highly likely that sales up to Joshuatmas will be much higher than other times of the year. This will make it harder to hit budget in some months than others.

The budget is based on the past. The past is, generally, a poor indicator of the future. Just because something was possible in year one it doesn't mean it is possible in year two. Staffing might have changed or levels competition might have increased meaning different targets are needed.

Controllability. Factory-wide costs are not under the control of production line managers so should not be included in their performance appraisal.

(b) | **General principles**

A budget revision should only be allowed if the budget contains an error (or poor estimate) that is outside the control of the business or the person upon which the budget is assigned.

It is important not to allow budget revisions for factors within the control of the business or the person being performance assessed. The risk here is that poor performance will essentially be 'blamed' on poor budgeting rather than weak operational actions.

In general the objective here is to end up with a fair and reasonable target that will properly motivate staff and managers.

Business rates increases

The business rates cost is entirely outside the control of production line managers so should not be included in their budgets or used for appraisal.

As far as the overall budget for the factory, the issue is whether the factory has been expanded or refurbished, then one could argue that the finance director chose to do that and so the increased cost was within their control. In this case a budget revision could not be supported. Any variance that resulted could instead be explained to senior management. However, if the local council have merely decided to collect more tax, then this is outside the control of the business and so a budget revision should be allowed.

> **Overtime**
>
> Much depends here on who decided to authorise the overtime and why it was incurred.
>
> If the board or Production Director instructed the production line managers concerned to pay overtime to hit production targets, then it was not under the control of the production line manager and a budget revision might be justified.
>
> On the other hand, if the production line made this decision, then the extra cost was within their control and no revision should be allowed – they should be held accountable for the overspend.

TASK 3

Weakness and effect thereof:

Weakness	Effect of Weakness
The **server location** is poor. It is unlikely that a standard office is that secure and so when Joshua is away the server is vulnerable. Equally a standard office might not be as fire protected or cooled, as a server room needs to be.	The server could be stolen (they are valuable) or otherwise damaged by fire or water. This could be accidental or deliberate. Equally access to it could be too free meaning that malicious software could be uploaded more easily than is desirable.
Back-ups of the programs themselves do not appear to be made nor does there appear to a replacement contract in place to replace a damaged server. (**Note:** The data backup system seems to be fine.)	In the event of damage the business could be disrupted for a longer period than in sensible. This could result in delayed processing of supplier payments or lost transactions as backlog occurs.
The **Password** system is poor. Leaving it up to staff to create passwords is risky, they will often take the line of least resistance creating easy to remember passwords rather than more secure versions.	Passwords could be guessed by 3rd parties or unauthorised other staff. This could mean data corruption or deliberate damage or even theft.
Copy invoices are sometimes processed on to the system. Only originals should be allowed.	Duplication could occur leading to duplicated payments. This also creates a culture that it is okay to bend the rules of the system, which could lead to other problems.
The **sales** data is processed in a cumbersome way, which presumably involves some manual reproduction of the data. Equally the batch header seems only to include a total for the number of invoices and no value total or other control totals (hash totals for example).	Data errors could be made which could mean the value of sales recorded does not tie in to what actually occurred.

TASK 4

Relevant cash flow principles

The principles behind the idea of relevant costing for decisions

When any decision is being made it can be difficult to determine exactly which figures should be incorporated and how significant they are. The principle behind relevant costing is that we only incorporate factors that are directly affected by the decision and to the extent that they are affected.

For an item to be included it should be:

- A future item: past costs and revenues are known as sunk and are ignored

- A cash flow: provisions, depreciations are not cash flow and should be excluded

- An incremental amount

    If, for example, we are comparing two possible outcomes:

    Cash position if we go ahead with the proposal   £A

    Cash position if we reject the proposal   £B

The relevant cash flow is the 'future incremental cash flow' and is the difference between the two outcomes = A – B

Comments of existing treatment:

Item	Comment on treatment
Research costs	These are sunk costs (past costs) and should be excluded from the appraisal.
Rent	The rent for the old factory will indeed be saved from the date the lease ends. When leases end there can also sometimes be extra payments to return the property to its original condition. These are called dilapidations and are relevant costs.
	However the new factory will presumably demand a rent payment and this should also be included.
Staff costs	The staff that relocate would have been paid anyway (in the old factory), so this cost is not relevant to the decision to move.
	Consequently the 20% calculation is also incorrect.
	Ruby Dale need to compare the wages before with the wages after the move to identify the relevant cash flow.
Equipment	Depreciation is not a cash flow and should be excluded.
	What is relevant here is the purchase cost of the new equipment (including installation) less the net realisable (i.e. scrap) value of the old fixtures if any.
Central allocated overhead	This is not relevant as there is no incremental cost at all.

	Cash flows incorrectly excluded (only ONE required)
1	The new equipment may result in other production cost savings that should be incorporated
2	The new equipment may result in higher quality, resulting in extra sales
3	Within staff costs it is hinted that some staff might take early redundancy. Redundancy payments will be relevant to the decision.
4	Given the change in location, there may be a change in distribution and transportation costs.

TASK 5

(a)   The ratios are as follows:

Gross profit %:	25,946/41,380	= 62.7%
Operating profit %	7,358/41,380	= 17.8%
Inventory holding period:	(3,780/15,434) × 365	= 89 days
Gearing	20,286/(20,286 + 36,836)	= 35.5%

(b)   With regard to complaints, which of the following statements is true?

The rate of complaints is up in all categories *The number of complaints is up in all categories but the **rate** of complaints with regard to late delivery is down slightly.* *X5 – rate = 4/800 = 0.50%* *X6 – rate = 4.3/925 = 0.46%*	X
Delivering on time is more important than delivering the right goods *Delivering the wrong goods even on time is just as much a mistake.*	X
The overall complaint rate is up 0.05% *This is correct:* *X5 – rate = (4 + 2)/800 = 0.75%* *X6 – rate = (4.3 + 3.1)/925 = 0.80%*	✓

(c) | **Interpretation of performance of "learning and training"**

The staff retention rate has fallen from 85% to 75%. Recruitment, development and retention of high quality staff are crucial to Ruby Dale's success, so this is a worrying trend. The implications for the business will include a loss of skills, additional recruitment and training costs, and an increased risk or errors and mistakes.

The lower % of staff undertaking apprenticeships, while resulting in cost savings, are also likely to result in lower skills, reduced loyalty and lower job satisfaction. This also goes against the firm's stated plans regarding sustainability.

Service based training has reduced by 10% points since 20X5 and this is perhaps unwise. This might indicate that the business has lost focus on the importance of service training.

The consequence of this is a reduced ability to 'service' the customers. Service is everything surrounding the product including serving customers in shops to delivery, invoicing and picking in the factory. This could result in lost sales in the future and a damaged reputation.

The above might explain the staff wellbeing figures. These are well down from 20X5 and perhaps poor levels of training might mean staff members feel a little 'unloved' by Ruby Dale.

Links to other categories on the balanced scorecard

A link could be made here to higher operating costs, as when staff members leave they will often have to be replaced particularly in this growing business. Recruitment costs can be significant; pushing up costs.

The link can be also made to the complaint rates. All the complaints issues seem to surround service levels. Late delivery and accuracy of delivery are up in absolute terms. This is perhaps where the business needs to focus, with extra training on the importance of these areas given and stricter targets enforced.

Invoicing errors are not as serious as in 20X5 and not as prevalent overall but complacency must be guarded against here.

TASK 6

Deficiencies	Controls
The wages calculations are generated by the payroll system and there are no checks performed. Therefore, if system errors occur during the payroll processing, this would not be identified. This could result in wages being over or under calculated, leading to an additional payroll cost or loss of employee goodwill.	A senior member of the payroll team should recalculate the gross to net pay workings for a sample of employees and compare their results to the output from the payroll system. These calculations should be signed as approved before payments are made.
Annual wages increases are updated in the payroll system standing data by clerks. Payroll clerks are not senior enough to be making changes to standing data as they could make mistakes leading to incorrect payment of wages. In addition, if they can access standing data, they could make unauthorised changes.	Payroll clerks should not have access to standing data changes within the system. The annual wages increase should be performed by a senior member of the payroll department and this should be checked by another responsible official for errors.
Overtime worked by employees is not all authorised by the relevant department head, as only overtime in excess of 30% of standard hours requires authorisation. This increases the risk that employees will claim for overtime even though they did not work these additional hours resulting in additional payroll costs for Ruby Dale.	All overtime hours worked should be authorised by the relevant department head. This should be evidenced by signature on the employees' weekly overtime sheets.

Deficiencies	Controls
Time taken off as payment for overtime worked should be agreed by payroll clerks to the overtime worked report; however, this has not always occurred. Employees could be taking unauthorised leave if they take time off but have not worked the required overtime.	Payroll clerks should be reminded of the procedures to be undertaken when processing the overtime sheets. They should sign as evidence on the overtime sheets that they have agreed any time taken off to the relevant overtime report.
The overtime worked report is emailed to the department heads and they report by exception if there are any errors. If department heads are busy or do not receive the email and do not report to payroll on time, then it will be assumed that the overtime report is correct even though there may be errors. This could result in the payroll department making incorrect overtime payments.	All department heads should report to the payroll department on whether or not the overtime report is correct. The payroll department should follow up on any non-replies and not make payments until agreed by the department head.
Department heads are meant to arrange for annual leave cover so that overtime sheets are authorised on a timely basis; however, this has not always happened. If overtime sheets are authorised late, then this can lead to employee dissatisfaction as it will delay payment of the overtime worked.	Department heads should be reminded of the procedures with regards to annual leave and arrangement of suitable cover. During annual leave periods, payroll clerks should monitor that overtime sheets are being submitted by department heads on a timely basis and follow up any late sheets.
The finance director reviews the total list of bank transfers with the total to be paid per the payroll records. There could be employees omitted along with fictitious employees added to the payment listing, so that although the total payments list agrees to payroll totals, there could be fraudulent payments being made.	The finance director when authorising the payments should on a sample basis perform checks from payroll records to payment list and vice versa to confirm that payments are complete and only made to bona fide employees. The finance director should sign the payments list as evidence that he has undertaken these checks.